# living
# on
# the
# edge
# of
# the
# world

New
Jersey
writers
take
on
the
Garden
State

Edited by **IRINA REYN**

**A TOUCHSTONE BOOK**    Published by Simon & Schuster   New York  London  Toronto  Sydney

TOUCHSTONE
Rockefeller Center
1230 Avenue of the Americas
New York, NY 10020

TOUCHSTONE and colophon are registered trademarks
of Simon & Schuster, Inc.

For information about special discounts for bulk purchases,
please contact Simon & Schuster Special Sales at
1-800-456-6798 or business@simonandschuster.com.

Designed by Jan Pisciotta

Manufactured in the United States of America

10   9   8   7   6   5   4   3   2   1

Library of Congress Cataloging-in-Publication Data

Living on the edge of the world : New Jersey writers take on the
    Garden State / edited by Irina Reyn.
       p. cm.
     "A Touchstone Book."
     1. American essays—21st century. 2. New Jersey—Social life
    and customs—Anecdotes. 3. Authors, American—Homes
    and haunts—New Jersey. 4. American essays—New Jersey.
    5. New Jersey—Biography—Anecdotes.  I. Reyn, Irina.
      PS548.N5L58  2007                              2007003412
      814'.6—dc22

ISBN-13: 978-0-7432-9160-6
ISBN-10:     0-7432-9160-3

For my parents, who brought me to New Jersey,
and for Adam, who always makes me appreciate it.

# CONTENTS

living

on

the

edge

of

the

world

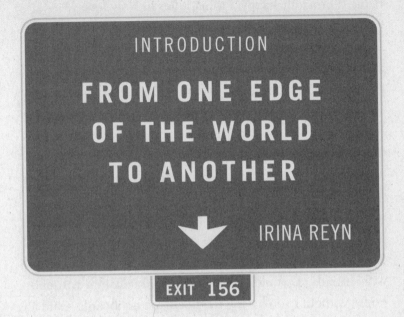

INTRODUCTION

# FROM ONE EDGE OF THE WORLD TO ANOTHER

IRINA REYN

EXIT 156

**W**hen I was seven years old, my parents and I emigrated from Moscow to Flatbush, Brooklyn. Two years later, just as I gained some confidence with the English language and began to grasp the geography of our new neighborhood, we relocated to Rego Park, Queens, where I began yet another elementary school. When I was almost fifteen, with one year at Forest Hills High School behind me, my parents announced that the three of us would be moving again—this time to Fair Lawn, New Jersey—so my father could start his own private medical practice. In my diary of that next major period of transition, I scribbled,

"There's something missing in my life that keeps me from being thoroughly happy. I think it lies in New Jersey."

Looking back on that diary entry now, it seems like the initial spark for *Living on the Edge of the World*: the first tentative steps toward imagining a literary New Jersey. This is the New Jersey I have strived to realize in this collection by collaborating with the writers gathered in these pages. But back then, I was exhausted from moving. I was longing for a place to rest, a safe place to discover myself. The anonymity of cities was all I knew, and my curiosity about the suburbs was fueled by powerful images from television. In the suburbs, I would have a shot at that elusive idyllic childhood, complete with a mother in the kitchen dispensing Oreos and Kool-Aid after impromptu soccer matches in the backyard with friends. I would be able to let myself into a friend's house without even having to knock, the cupboards—and all their decadent, artificially flavored contents—available to me any time of day.

The dreams were simple, naive, almost regressive, an attempt to recapture a childhood I never had. Mainly, though, I was drawn to the stability of those suburban images: houses lived in throughout entire lifetimes, no switching of schools, no packing up of apartments, no learning of a new language, no painstaking process of turning strangers into friends. What I was searching for in New Jersey was the impossible: a perfectly cohesive sense of home.

The New Jersey I discovered had little in common with my suburban fantasies. The first year in New Jersey was almost as much of a culture shock as my first years in the United States. I was bewildered by malls, by their mysterious lack of function, where you went not to shop but simply to walk around in aimless circles, to see and be seen. I didn't . know what to make of the genre of slicked-back student referred to by others as the "Guido"—with the fuzzy dice hanging from his car's rearview mirror, the lights around the license plate flashing, the car bopping up and down to Z100 at red lights. Diners, although off-putting at first for their gaudy, downscale Art Deco furnishings and indifferent service, became a comforting, reliable dispenser of late-night coffee, rice pudding, cheese sticks, and cherry pie (heated, of course, and with ice cream). In New Jersey, it seemed, I was an immigrant all over again.

I found nighttime in Fair Lawn silent and eerie and was convinced I smelled toxic waste everywhere (a city girl not realizing that the scent was actually emanating from skunks rather than the New Jersey equivalent of Chernobyl). Other than the twenty-four-hour CVS, a diner or two, a Friendly's, and a Baskin-Robbins, there was little of interest in walking distance. I missed apartment buildings, with their noises, their smells, the palpable proximity of other human bodies. As the paint dried, as the new furniture began to occupy the space it still does to this day, I yearned to tell my parents they had made a mistake.

But time passed, and like it or not, I was maturing in New Jersey. It was in Fair Lawn where I experienced my first boyfriend (and lost him to another girl three months later), where I learned to drive (and backed the car into the tree adjoining our driveway my first day behind the wheel). Where I discovered acting in school plays (but not yet the fact that I was a terrible actress). Where I watched my father attain the goals a Jewish man could never have realized in Russia, including the establishment of a flourishing private practice. Where I honed my skills of observation, edging closer to becoming a writer.

Another major event occurred in our household, a year before I left Fair Lawn for college—my parents gave birth to my sister, Elizabeth. Now, sixteen years later, she is as old as I was when I moved to Fair Lawn. She has lived in the same house since she was born and has the same group of friends she had since she was a toddler. She is the real deal, a bona fide New Jerseyan.

Buying the Fair Lawn house was my parents' biggest investment in America, so my own immigrant guilt narrowed my choices for higher education to a single school: Rutgers, the State University of New Jersey. With its central campus located in New Brunswick, an hour south of Fair Lawn, Rutgers attracted primarily in-state students. Many Rutgers students were thrilled to be attending the school, but there were others who felt they had few choices about where to go to college or had hoped to get out of New Jersey but resigned themselves to the low tuition and high-quality education Rutgers offered. It was there, in the River dorms, the classrooms, while strolling the green esplanade of Voorhees Mall, or over a "Mexican Cantina" dinner in the cavernous dining hall, that I met people from all over the state. Eventually, my understanding of New Jersey widened; Rutgers is where I learned about the state's diversity, its regional personalities, its multicultural communities.

"What's your exit?" I was asked again and again by students

seeking to understand me, to draw conclusions about me from the magical number that would summarize my background. So I learned to explain myself by my exit off the New Jersey Turnpike (18W) and Garden State Parkway (156), but of course it was hardly my entire story. It was at Rutgers where I first realized that many New Jerseyans had a sheepish relation to their own state; when asked by outsiders where they were from, some of the students said they hailed from "the New York area" or perhaps just "New York." For me it was even more complicated. I was a Russian Jew who lived in New York and New Jersey—Moscow straddling both sides of the Hudson.

This fractured identity allowed me a view of New Jersey that spurred the creation of this book. My loyalties being divided, I was able to examine the state from without and within. What I eventually found was something much more familiar than what I originally confronted in the back of a Fair Lawn High School classroom, lost in the mist of Aqua Net, intimidated by the girls' hazardously long fingernails, their pleated Z. Cavaricci pants. What I discovered after some time and distance was a state I could relate to, a state whose self-regard was as confusing as my own.

If I started to recognize myself in New Jersey, then I've also had the opportunity to see New Jersey become like me. In the years since my parents moved to Fair Lawn, the town's population has changed—the Russians have moved in. The town now has three Russian supermarkets, and across the street from the largest of these is a Russian pharmacy that imports products from Moscow, St. Petersburg, and Warsaw.

In the heart of the town, the local video store stocks tapes of Russian movies that never received U.S. distribution. Just a few blocks away, on Fair Lawn Avenue, a former Lions Club has been transformed into an Orthodox Jewish synagogue, where the services are conducted entirely in Russian. And just minutes away by car are at least two sprawling Russian restaurants, where families celebrate weddings, birthdays, and anniversaries, where they dance, make vodka toasts, and eat grilled shashlik. Fair Lawn has become dear to me over the years, finally taking shape as the first place I've known that resembles home.

Since New Jersey is the place where I experienced my first glimmers of true self-recognition, it is the place that will always fascinate me, with its mass of contradictions I am still trying to untangle. New Jersey may be the nation's punching bag, the butt of countless jokes, yet the density of its population makes it a unique world of its own (at approximately 1,165 people per square mile, it is more densely populated than any other state). New Jersey's per capita income is the second highest in the country, and it can be considered one of our most ethnically diverse states. Strangely enough, none of these statistics staunches the flow of Jersey jokes.

New Jersey's role in movies and other forms of popular culture suggests that the country has an emotional investment in perpetuating the state's browbeaten reputation, as though New Jersey were the hidden self we want to degrade and protect, simultaneously. I was reminded of this while watching Sandra Bullock in *Miss Congeniality*, where the actress plays an undercover FBI agent who enters a Miss America–type beauty pageant. The fact that Bullock's initially unglamorous and hilariously klutzy Gracie Hart enrolls in the contest as Miss New Jersey is no coincidence. What could be a funnier state than New Jersey? At the same time, what state could be more authentic? Gracie Hart, after all, is the only "real" person in a pageant extolling artificiality, whose kindness and common sense the contestants from other states come to depend upon. Perhaps that is part of New Jersey's responsibility—to act as the underdog the country jeers but privately longs to root for. We want to believe that even when you dress up New Jersey, its grittiness will always shine through—for better and for worse. This is the double-edged myth that exerts such a powerful hold on our national psyche.

Still, the Garden State's most complicated relationship remains with its larger-than-life neighbor to the east, and, like the less-favored sibling, its feelings about New York City are multifaceted—ambivalent, fiercely proud, insecure, somewhat defensive. Like me, New Jersey embodies a kind of placelessness, a spiritual disconnection from itself, its identity constantly in question. (A case in point was the recent search for a state slogan. The governor discarded an out-of-state public relations firm's suggestion, "New Jersey: We'll Win You Over," for the more optimistic "New Jersey: See for Yourself." Now even this slogan has been eliminated for its lack of originality.) Yet hasn't there always been something valuable about being on the margins, forced to monitor the center from a self-conscious distance? Perhaps one might even imagine such a vantage point as a literary one.

Since college, I have tried to grasp the essence of New Jersey by immersing myself in contemporary Jersey culture. I bought albums by Bruce Springsteen, then Bon Jovi, then Fountains of Wayne, then My Chemical Romance. I watched a miniboom of films set in New Jersey, including *Jersey Girl, Garden State,* and *Harold & Kumar Go to White Castle.* I tuned in to *The Sopranos.* I eagerly followed the evolution of the *Weird N.J.* 'zine, with its accounts of uncanny roadside attractions, outlandish architectural landmarks, and all other kinds of bizarre Jersey phenomena. *Weird N.J.* has since grown into a franchise and book series that is sold across the country, showing how the quirkiness of the Garden State can apparently lend itself to larger, even national, meanings.

Alongside the music, films, and magazines that identified themselves with New Jersey, I also became aware of contemporary writers mining New Jersey as a rich subject for their books. New Jersey writing has a long history of its own, with William Carlos Williams, Robert Pinsky, Philip Roth, Richard Ford, Alicia Ostriker, and Amiri Baraka among its literary lions, but all around me, a new generation of writers was drawing its inspiration from the Garden State. I have invited them to lend their voices to this nonfiction collection, and the result is a variety of different New Jerseys, each filtered through singular experiences in the Garden State. At the same time, though, the authors share certain themes that illuminate one another and show us what it means to live in New Jersey.

This collection includes stories of unexpected discovery, of finding meaning in unlikely places. Joshua Braff writes about running into his high school crush later in life, and he finds in her a mesmerizing, grown-up version of the Jersey Girl of his youth. David Roth discovers a different love, a borderline criminal passion for the then-beleaguered New Jersey Nets. Elizabeth Keenan uncovers something much more frightening just weeks before the death of her best friend—the possibility of an actual encounter with the mythical Jersey Devil.

Almost all of the writers grew up in New Jersey, so it should be no surprise that the book features tales of awkward, transcendent adolescent sex. Jonathan Ames's teenage Jersey shore fantasy slips away within inches of his grasp—or does it? Askold Melnyczuk recalls becoming both a student and a teacher of sex in a Cranford quasi-triple-decker house stuffed with Ukrainian immigrants.

There are stories of New Jersey as threatening and dangerous. Frederick Reiken confronts a mobster's son in Fort Lee. James Kaplan finds himself drawn to the suicide of the West Orange mobster Longy Zwillman. Gaiutra Bahadur's family of Guyanese immigrants lives in fear of being targeted by the "Dotbusters," a racist gang intent on driving the Indian community out of Jersey City. Dani Shapiro's Orthodox Jewish family also receives a chilly reception in Hillside circa 1963.

Aching loss permeates a number of these essays. Kathleen DeMarco's family is forced to sell their beloved cranberry farm in Hammonton. Caren Lissner copes with the end of her parents' marriage by living in a car and working at the Jackson amusement park Great Adventure.

Some authors who tried hard to get out of New Jersey found that it haunted their work. Lucinda Rosenfeld, Tom Perrotta, and Cathi Hanauer all came to realize from afar that New Jersey offers the most resonant and recurring setting for their fiction. Adam Lowenstein left his hometown to become a professor of film studies but finds himself fascinated by New Jersey cinema.

And then there are tales of coming home. Christian Bauman recounts the pleasure of a daily commute on the PATH train between New York and Hoboken. Caroline Leavitt copes with the public disapproval of her new neighbors, longtime Hoboken residents wary of infiltration by Manhattan refugees in search of cheaper housing. And there is Lauren Grodstein, a prodigal daughter who leaves Haworth only to return to New Jersey as a professor at Rutgers University's Camden campus.

As we traverse this literary version of the New Jersey Turnpike, through the eighteen "exits" that form the chapters of this anthology, each story paints a dynamic and complex picture of New Jersey as both state and state of mind. The essays move beyond outsiders' knee-jerk assumptions about a state glimpsed from the windows of cars and trains leaving Newark Liberty International Airport on their way to somewhere else. These writers reckon with the commodification, disdain, and disregard attached to New Jersey, but they are ultimately interested in something far more intimate, something truly lived.

*Living on the Edge of the World* is not meant to be a simple rallying cry of a book, a manifesto determined to convince the reader why New Jersey matters. In fact, the author biographies included in this volume reveal that only three of the contributors currently live in New Jersey. This calls to mind a story a friend of mine once told me. Born and raised in New Jersey, he went away to college out of state and introduced himself to his new roommate, who hailed from Colorado. He expected the usual "armpit-of-America" response once he informed him where he had grown up, but his roommate surprised him. He said, "You know why they call it the Garden State, don't you? It's like the Garden of Eden—everyone is from there originally, but no one you meet actually lives there anymore." The mythic observation of this story seems to hover over *Living on the Edge of the World*.

No one book could possibly hope to cover all of New Jersey's unique places, people, and communities—I wish I could have included essays on Atlantic City, Asbury Park, Cape May, Newark, Paterson, Trenton, or any number of other notable locales. I would have liked to publish more writers from New Jersey's myriad ethnic communities. I would have loved to come across a meditation on Jon Bon Jovi's hair. Nevertheless, I hope this book captures the spirit of the state as it brings together the very best in contemporary New Jersey writing.

No essay in this book focuses entirely on Bruce Springsteen (although he does surface in some of the contributors' essays), but the title of this collection speaks to the pervasive influence his work has had for the state of New Jersey. For me, no song captures the Garden State's essence of hope and desolation (as stubbornly local as it is universal) better than Springsteen's "Living on the Edge of the World," with its passionate, desperate narrator crisscrossing the highways of New Jersey:

> *Radio, radio, hear my tale of heartbreak*
> *New Jersey in the morning like a lunar landscape.*

When I wrote that diary entry as a girl in New York City days before moving to New Jersey, I thought I would find my home on the other side of the Hudson River. That did not happen the way I envisioned it, but what I found there instead was a home within my homelessness. The "edge of the world," it seems, turned out to be more essential, more invigorating than any center could have been.

So I hope this collection speaks to the reader's own experiences of living on the edge of the world, no matter where you come from.

*Fair Lawn, New Jersey,*
*and Brooklyn, New York, 2005–2006*

# THE FAMILY FARM

## KATHLEEN DEMARCO

EXIT 7

n September 2004, I stood with my husband, my three-month-old son, and my older brother as I listened to a speaker at the dedication ceremony for the Franklin Parker Preserve, a ten-thousand-acre tract of land in the middle of the New Jersey Pine Barrens. It was a slightly overcast, humid day, but most of the two hundred people attending this ceremony were jubilant; the purchase of this property by a nonprofit conservation group had been confirmed, and now this land would be preserved for time immemorial—for, as the speaker was saying, "future generations of Parkers to come and play" in in the years ahead. I had gone to college and was friends with John Parker, Franklin Parker's son and the person who had dedicated much of his time to raising the funds the organization needed to purchase this land. That he, on the organization's behalf, had purchased this land from my father, uncle, and aunt was a fact I had been unwilling to accept. But on this day I had no choice but to acknowledge the sale. We were standing on a field where I had picked blueberries every year of my young childhood, when this field had been part of the blueberry and cranberry farm that had been owned and operated by my family for sixty-two years. Perhaps this, more than anything, made it clear that my childhood—and childish—assumptions of inheritance and family ties were, at best, naive. Standing there, I felt like I did when I saw a dead person in a casket—the farm was dead, really dead, and this left me feeling anything but jubilant.

This, then, is a story about the life of a family farm, and its death.

From 1941 until 2003, my family owned a cranberry farm in southern New Jersey. (Forget quaint notions of a farm with chickens and pigs, a couple of bogs, and a nice old man with a pitchfork. This was a major agribusiness, one of the largest such farms in the United States.) I should stop here and say that there's no point in explaining (yet again) that New Jersey accommodates more than the stereotypical turnpikes and smokestacks and unfulfilled New York City wannabes; if you don't know there's a 1.1-million acre stretch of federally protected, mostly undeveloped land between Philadelphia and

Atlantic City—a place where the majority of the population couldn't care less about New York City—you should perhaps consider a trip to this place called the Pine Barrens and prepare to be amazed.

My grandfather, Anthony R. DeMarco, didn't have time to be amazed. As trite as it sounds, he had a dream, and he pursued it. In 1941 he purchased about 6,500 acres of land in southern New Jersey from another man of Italian heritage, Prince Mario Ruspoli di Poggio Suasa. Prince Ruspoli was an attaché at the Italian Embassy in Washington, D.C. My grandfather was a New Jersey–born pharmacist who had grown up working on cranberry and blueberry farms in southern New Jersey. He and his siblings had worked on the farms as part of crews assembled by his father, my great-grandfather, Rocco DeMarco. Rocco DeMarco had emigrated from Italy with his two brothers and had become a *padrone*—a man responsible for bringing crews of Italian men to work on the farms in southern New Jersey. He had settled in Hammonton, New Jersey, a place that currently has not one, but two, claims to national fame. First, it is the town with the most Italian Americans per square inch in the country. (Apparently 53 percent of my hometown population represented themselves as Italian American in the 2000 U.S. census, more than any other place with a population of more than 1,000 people.) And second, it is the "Blueberry Capital of the World"—i.e., the place where the most blueberries are grown anywhere on the globe. Check the packaging of the next pint of blueberries you buy. HAMMONTON, NEW JERSEY, will most likely be the place of origin. Hammonton has had a stable population of about 11,000 people for more than a hundred years; it is a veritable city next to the town of Chatsworth, about twenty-eight miles northeast traveling on Route 206, with a population of about 1,200. This is probably why my great-grandfather, apparently something of a ladies' man, settled in Hammonton and not Chatsworth. My grandfather, on the other hand, traveled between Hammonton and Chatsworth for most of his adult life, especially once he met his wife.

My grandmother, Gladys Alloway DeMarco, was a schoolteacher from Friendship, New Jersey, a place of only about fourteen homes, situated in between Hammonton and Chatsworth. My grandmother's family—decidedly non-Italian—could trace their American roots back to the time when their ancestor William Alloways was the scrivener to William Penn. My grandmother's father, Garfield Alloway, was the manager of another cranberry farm in the Pine Barrens, Evans & Wills. He had met my grandfather when the latter had worked as a laborer at Evans & Wills. I have no idea what Garfield Alloway thought when his daughter Gladys married Tony DeMarco—I only know the story that when my grandfather showed up at the door, my grandmother's relatives would yell, "Gladie! The dago's here!" Still, discrimination against Italians only spurred my grandfather on to bigger and more ambitious behavior. If he wanted to do something like, say, buy thousands of acres of land, that's exactly what he would do.

By 1941, Prince Ruspoli had decided to return to Europe. His masterpiece—a resort called the Chatsworth Club, whose members included Astors, du Ponts, Morgans, and Vanderbilts—had burned down in the late 1930s, and this, along with the aftereffects of the Great Depression and the burgeoning world war, convinced him it was time to leave New Jersey. Through his lawyers, he sold his property to my grandfather for $100,000.

My grandfather's total net worth at the time was about $1,000, if we're being generous. According to my father, my grandfather felt his $100,000 mortgage was justified in that a complete loss would leave him with nothing, which is what he had when he made the deal in the first place. It seems doubtful, however, that my grandfather believed he would end up with nothing. The land he purchased was full of eco-logical treasures—pine forests and untainted water and the as-yet-unnamed Pine Barrens tree frog, among countless other animals and plants. This is important information now, since all of these sites and species will be protected by the conservation group, but I don't have a clue whether my grandfather cared particularly about any of these creatures or plants—he died before I was born. What I do suspect he cared about was another naturally occurring element on his new property: cranberries. And not just cranberries—blue-berries, too. In fact, it seems as if my grandfather had a broad vision for himself once he shrugged off his pharmaceutical career and became a farmer and, perhaps more important, a landowner. By all accounts he worked constantly, as if driven by a passion usually associated with athletes or artists—or, perhaps, poor men with great ambition. Every day he trav-eled the twenty-eight miles to Chatsworth, supervising all parts of his growing businesses before driving home to Ham-monton, to his wife and family. Indeed, he did this every day up to and including the day he was killed by a drunk driver in a car accident, December 31, 1964.

By the time he died, Anthony R. DeMarco had paid off his mortgage, created a thriving blueberry and cranberry farm, built up and managed a vast produce brokerage that brought New Jersey–grown fruits and vegetables to consumers around the country, and started a trucking company that was responsible for bringing the first flats of New Jersey blueberries to markets west of the Mississippi River. During this time he had also invented a hybrid form of cranberry, called the cropper, that is still cultivated today. Finally, and perhaps most notably, he joined a fledgling cooperative of cranberry farmers based in Massachusetts. The cooperative was called Ocean Spray. Unfortunately for my grandfather, he did not live long enough to bear the real financial fruits of his multienterprises. That was for the next generation.

In a Horatio Alger version of the American Dream, my grandfather's three children all attended Ivy League colleges and/or graduate schools and became just as well trained in economics as they were knowledgeable about farming in New Jersey. They also, as the American Dream goes, were exposed to the Other World outside New Jersey. New influences flooded their lives, and, as in many similar families, the desire of the next generation to leave their hometown and explore new terrain was pronounced. This was true of my uncle and aunt, although my father had chosen to return to Hammonton as a lawyer and a family man. My aunt did move away, living first in Pittsburgh and then further west, in Idaho and Washington. My uncle, who has stated he wished he could have moved to a city like San Francisco after graduating from Yale Law School, was instead named the manager of my grandfather's business after my grandfather's untimely death. He became a superb operational manager, and, as Ocean Spray prospered, so did our cranberry farm.

Permit me to write about cranberry farming from the perspective of an observer—someone who never rode a tractor, churned up the berries, or went anywhere near the perilous beehives spotted around the property. At the risk of espousing hyperbole, cranberry farming is, without exception, the most extraordinary agricultural spectacle in the world. The cranberry harvest in New Jersey occurs during the fall, usually during the month of October. On our farm's property of pitch pines and streams and frogs, there were six hundred acres of cultivated cranberry bogs, situated amid the tall white pine and red cedar trees and adjacent to green lakes of "cedar water." Cranberry farming is an example of a crop that is respectful of the environment; it is a crop that grows no matter what, whether in a cultivated bog or in its cousin, the ignominious swamp. Pesticide and fertilizer use is minimal, and the water used in the harvest is pristine, unharmed by the cranberry farming that has been occurring naturally for more than one hundred years. The bogs, which for the summer months are literal carpets of tangled cranberry vines, are flooded via a system of dams, such that the vines themselves are swallowed up by the water. Specialized machines—think tractors for water—are then driven through the bogs by farmworkers who know the correct paths to avoid damage to the vines, and the berries are shaken off the vines so that they float to the top. Consider, then, the sight: red cranberries atop a small lake of blue water, encircled by evergreen trees and—if you're lucky—under an idyllic blue autumnal sky. Extraordinary.

(It should be noted that the sight of a cranberry harvest is about as far away from the conventional perception of New Jersey as the moon is from Newark. If you aren't moved by the sight of a cranberry harvest, perhaps you'll be moved by the metaphorical collapse of the New Jersey stereotype. There is no turnpike here.)

After the cranberries tumble from the vines and rise to the surface of the water, they are collected via transportable conveyor systems to a dump truck waiting alongside the bog. In our farm's case, the cranberries were then taken to the Ocean Spray processing plant in nearby Bordentown, New Jersey, where they eventually became part of the vast array of juices available on your grocery shelves.

After the harvest, the bogs remain flooded throughout the winter so that the water protects the cranberry vines from freezing. If, on wintry nights, the temperature threatens to destroy the vines, resident farmworkers stay on the bogs throughout the night, irrigating them so the water stays fluid. In the spring the bogs are drained, the bees are put into service, and the cycle of cranberry farming begins anew.

I never worked on the farm during the cranberry harvest. But my mother insisted that my three siblings and I work on our family's blueberry farm during our childhood summers. My mother had grown up in Malaga, New Jersey, a tiny town of about 800 located about fifteen miles from my hometown of Hammonton. One of ten children, her Italian immigrant father and American-born Italian mother stressed the need for education above all else, and she put herself through college and graduate school and (she swears) would have finished her Ph.D. dissertation if she hadn't been rudely interrupted by marriage and the subsequent arrival of four children within five years. No matter; in her heart she is and always will be a farm girl. She remembers cutting laurel in the winters and picking turnips and beets and strawberries in the summer, and will recount (ad nauseam, if I'm to be truthful) how hard she worked in the fields from some obscenely young age. It was not surprising, then, that she brought her own four children to her husband's farm at a similarly obscenely young age, first to pick blueberries and then to work either in the farm's concrete shed as a packer (my sister and I) or in the fields driving trucks (my brothers). Sometimes, when she travels to visit me in Manhattan, my mother looks out the window and shudders. "I need space," she says, "I like to know there are farms around." I feel the same thing.

Still, my mother—who had taken a giant step away from her mother's life when she finished high school, then college, then graduate school—pushed her children to take even further giant steps away from her. She was the one who decided that her children needed to leave the Hammonton public school system to go away to boarding school; she—a woman supremely comfortable in the environs of South Jersey—was the one who intimated the idea that there was a larger world available to us, even if it meant, however unacknowledged, losing her children to that same larger world. This is why, in the fall of 1982, I found myself at St. Andrew's School in Middletown, Delaware, a coed boarding-only high school so impressively preppy that it later served as the setting for the film *Dead Poets Society*.

When I left Hammonton for St. Andrew's, I didn't know many things. For starters, I had no idea that New Jersey's nickname, the Garden State, was a joke to most of the outside world. This was a bit of a problem, since by the time you're fifteen you're supposed to know what's a joke and what isn't, especially if it's about the place where you've spent fifteen years. But there, on Delaware soil, in front of a girl who had just told me (not a bit nicely) that her grandfather was one of New England's finest poets, I stood, dumb as a post, when she laughed after I told her I was from New Jersey. "The Garden State," she said with a lisp. "All the chemicals you can buy."

In retrospect, this was the first of many times when I felt that I knew very little about my home state. In boarding school, things were different. Not everyone's name ended in a vowel. Not everyone came from or worked on a farm. Everyone—well, mostly everyone—did seem to have an impression of New Jersey (and Italians, for that matter), and it wasn't good. (To interrupt some naysayers, I know there are people who say that the big-haired, stupid, criminal, New Jersey–Italian stereotype *is* good, at least in an "isn't it dramatic/funny/passionate" way. They're wrong.) But perhaps what made me most different from my peers was the fact that I had recently been named the 1982 New Jersey Blueberry Queen.

In Hammonton, the Blueberry Queen was like Homecoming Queen, chosen from among the many girls who worked on blueberry farms during the summer. Since everyone did work for a farm, the only other requirement, just as for Prom Queen or Homecoming Queen, was to be attractive and popular. I was certainly happy I had won—it's always better to win, after all—but what I remember most about that night was that my overprotective parents had not allowed me to take a date to the event. But I didn't think winning a contest based on congeniality, and yes, beauty, was necessarily something of which to be embarrassed. So I told some people at my new school. Mistake. At boarding school, Blueberry Queen was like Resident New Girl Freak. (Or so I thought. I've since discovered that some of my peers genuinely believed my title was quaint and appealingly authentic.) And Blueberry Queen of *New Jersey*? I might as well have just set myself up in the school common with a bull's-eye on my back. After all, it was bad enough that I had a surfeit of knowledge about farming; that the farming occurred in New Jersey was a peculiarity so strange and so unexpected that I'm certain my classmates and teachers wondered whether I was lying. (Much later, my British editor, upon receiving the manuscript of my first novel, *Cranberry Queen*, asked me if I had invented the Pine Barrens, much as Lewis Carroll had done with Alice and her Wonderland.)

To a fifteen-year-old girl with a big smile and weak psyche, the gap between what I knew to be true and what my new peers knew to be true was wide and deep. I was Blueberry Queen of New Jersey; my new roommate had just returned from an Outward Bound trip where she had pranced around nude for three days. I spent my summers working on a farm; my new peers spent their summers at camps where they learned how to kayak and play tennis. I had no idea how to navigate this big pond in which I was the proverbially small fish. So I did something fairly challenging for a teenager: I realized the social value of being from a different background so long as I acted the same as everyone else. This meant wearing clothes that were too big, retaining the hard "g" sound at the end of gerunds, and, most notably, using my grandfather's prescience at becoming a member of Ocean Spray to prove that I was not so different from my tennis-playing peers.

But here's the weird part. I wasn't lying. By the time I attended St. Andrew's, Ocean Spray had hit its stride. The crop called "red gold" by the media had, under Ocean Spray's manipulations, transformed itself into juices so desired by the public that the Ocean Spray brand had become synonymous with fresh, healthy good taste. It was doing so well that it was increasing its price, eventually paying its members, the growers, approximately $60 per barrel. Our farm produced more than one hundred thousand barrels annually. Do the math: this was indeed a prosperous time.

All of my peers had heard of Ocean Spray, and in the social currency of boarding school and the Ivy League, this was what was important. (It may not be surprising to learn that what was most notable about Ocean Spray, at least to my classmates, was that cranberry juice was rumored to soothe urinary tract infections and, perhaps more important, was a necessary ingredient for a Sea Breeze.) Yes, I was a naive farm girl from a part of New Jersey no one knew about, but no, I was not naive enough to think that people wouldn't be impressed by my family's business. The fact that the business succeeded on the tiny backs of a beautiful homegrown crop only added to the charm; I was an heiress to a cranberry empire, and this was a very formidable social mallet to wield. That the "estate" in which I would undoubtedly share at some point in my future was an agricultural marvel, respectful of the environment, and lucrative was a further bonus. I deduced an inclination of my new peers to look at my background with a quaintness not necessarily deserved and used it to my advantage. Blueberry Queen of New Jersey, I realized, indicated to some people a certain country-rube flavor, and while this initially embarrassed me, it later helped me write about people who couldn't see beyond the obvious. (Or in my case, the tiara. Remember this the next time you see a pleasant-looking farm girl; she may be figuring out how to use you as a character in her next book.)

The one given in the story I had created for myself and my background was the farm itself. It had never occurred to me that my siblings and I, as well as my aunt's daughter, would not, at some point in the distant future, run the farm. In the first place, it just made sense: hadn't my grandfather handed over the reins to his children? Perhaps more important, the operation was in amazing shape—so efficient that it was the highest-producing-per-acre farm in the entire Ocean Spray cooperative. It was inconceivable that the farm would not continue, not just for my children but for my children's children, and so long as the market prevailed.

But then the market failed, however briefly. And not only the market. My family did, too.

The market first. By the late 1990s, Ocean Spray's prices had dropped to $17 a barrel due to oversupply, and Ocean Spray was in free fall. During this time there had been a chance for Ocean Spray to merge with one of the huge, multinational beverage corporations, but the board of directors, fundamentally a group of independent-minded farmers, had narrowly voted it down, choosing instead to wait out this blow by the market system until supply again met demand. My family had lobbied hard for the merger, and for my uncle, a member of the board of directors and a seasoned and extraordinarily successful politician in his own right, this loss must have been bitter.

And then my family—my father, that is, and his brother and sister—collided over the fiscal management of the farm. In the 1990s and then again in 2003, my father sued my uncle over his fiscal management of the farm, alleging in his suits that the debt incurred by the farm under my uncle's management was the reason the farm needed to be sold. My uncle denied any wrongdoing in his management of the farm and was quoted in the press during 2003 as saying he had sold the farm because "the cranberry industry has inalterably changed. Cranberry farming is just not profitable, and I don't see it changing anytime soon." (It is worth noting that Ocean Spray reported a 40 percent revenue growth in 2004.)

Both cases were settled before a court trial, putting a legal end to both the farm and my grandfather's businesses. It is impossible to end childhood memories, however, which means that there will be no settling of disconcerting emotions with respect to my family. My father's siblings were extraordinarily close to my siblings and myself; it is not a stretch to say that I would not have been a writer today if not for them. I had hoped—rather naively—that all this family squabbling would end up in a compromise, however untidy. But in hindsight, my optimism seems baseless. All the signs of an impending sale were there. My older brother used to say, "Kathy, write it off. It's gone." It was my choice to ignore the war brewing in my father's generation; like a ridiculous

Pollyanna, I always thought that these very smart people would figure out some way to keep the farm in our family, market forces—and even lawsuits—be damned.

But then the sale to the conservation group closed, on December 31, 2003.

As should be obvious by now, I assumed the farm was as much a part of me as my head. I never personally owned a shard of the land, of course, and during the school year it was rare for me even to visit the property—except when I wanted to brag to friends, in which case I brought them to south Jersey to witness the harvest for themselves. On those days, when we would leave looking around the vast property, extending as far as we could see in all directions, I would feel inordinately proud: *Look what my grandfather did! Look at what my family has!* Of course, my actual physical knowledge of the cranberry farm was abstract—when I took a boyfriend to the fields for the first time, I mistakenly showed him the immaculately groomed cranberry bogs of the Lee Brothers Farm, a farm adjacent to our own, before I realized my mistake. But I knew the blueberry fields—or at least where the blueberry fields were. I tried to show this boyfriend the fields where I had first picked, way back in the early 1970s, but the gate was locked, and the rusted PROPERTY OF A. R. DEMARCO ENTERPRISES sign was hanging by one link of a corroded chain. Thwarted, I still showed him other childhood places: the lake once adorned by Prince Ruspoli's Chatsworth Club; the corner store where I had used my blueberry-picking earnings to buy red string licorice. I made us drive down the paved roads and the dirt paths where I used to go motorbike riding when I was a teenager, and I showed him the local municipal building, named for my grandparents, located on the one main street of this very small town. I showed him the Ocean Spray processing plant, and I basically bragged all the way back to New York City about my family, my grandfather, my life, myself.

For a long while, I didn't know that my attachment to the property was so extravagant—I didn't realize that the summer months of my childhood accumulated to an aggregate, intangible relationship, one that enriches me as a person even as I still straddle the gap between my upbringing in South Jersey and life in Every Place Else. It is not a coincidence that I write most easily about New Jersey, *my* New Jersey; it is no surprise that the mythology I created because of my time spent on the farm is the well to which I return again and again when I approach my fiction.

Many times since the sale has been concluded I've comforted myself with this (banal) train of thought: "What is ownership, anyway? Who can *own* anything?" This helps only a little. And the money? I suppose people may think the $12 million sale price would temper much of the grief—this is not true, and not only because there will not be much (if any) of the $12 million left. (Banks and lawyers seem in some way to be the ones most benefiting from my grandfather's vision.) And then there is one more thing that adds to the hurt feelings, the mourning. After the sale closed, it was reported in the press that none of my generation was interested in running the farm. This, insofar as it represents my siblings and myself, is not true. If any of us had been asked, the answer would have been yes.

And so, at last, we're back at the dedication ceremony for the Franklin Parker Preserve, formerly the land owned by my father, uncle, and aunt, formerly the land owned by Prince Ruspoli, formerly the land lived on by the Leni Lenape Indians, formerly the land not owned by anyone. We stand on the blueberry field whose gate had been locked years earlier, when I took my then boyfriend, now husband to see it. My son, squirming at my chest, will have no memory of this day. Sophie Parker, my friend John's youngest child, may—she is off in the distance, a beautiful girl playing on the vast field where I used to work. I envision future generations of Parkers playing on this same field, just as the speaker is predicting, and I suddenly feel the tether connecting me to the Pine Barrens snap. At that precise moment, I silently vow that I will never return, that I will never take my children to this place, that if family heritage means nothing to my family, then my children have no reason to have any ties to this place. (And really, who cares if any of this proves to be true? My place will be eagerly taken by the visitors who will come to the Franklin Parker Preserve, excited to explore and canoe and hike and see this stunning wilderness in the state where unsightliness is presumed.) I will continue to use the farm, and its mysterious New Jersey setting, as inspiration for my fiction, because I seem unable to do otherwise, but I will not come to see it, not anymore. And I will continue to look for other reasons why this farm no longer exists—environmentalists, Ocean Spray's management, the Pine Barrens tree frog—while I deliberately avoid what I know to be the truth: that a family, like a farm, cannot, ultimately, retain perfect control of its crop, no matter how cultivated the produce and no matter how much it is beloved.

# ROSE OF THE JERSEY SHORE

## JONATHAN AMES

EXIT 82

I was eighteen, and in the middle of July of 1982, I was down at Seaside Park, New Jersey, for the weekend. A friend and I had rented a twenty-dollar-a-day room overlooking the boardwalk, the beach, and the ocean. We were on top of Mike's Clam on the Half-Shell, and the smells were perfect for the Jersey shore: frying grease, old fish, and ocean breeze.

We lay on the beach sunburning ourselves all day on Saturday, and then, late in the afternoon, we went to our room and drank beer, which I had managed to buy with my older sister's doctored driver's license (I had changed her name from Donna to Donald).

Our room had one big double bed, and we sat on it and wiped our sandy feet along the walls. Many others had done this before us, and the walls were covered with footprints.

Around my fourth beer, I was feeling pretty good and I leaned my head out the window and I saw two girls walking up the boardwalk in that beautiful six-o'clock-in-the-evening sunlight. They were wearing tank tops and their shoulders were dark brown and they had trim teenage figures.

"You want to drink some beer?" I called out to them.

I was expecting to get the finger.

"Sure," one of them called out.

"You do? . . . Well, come on up!" I said, and I pointed at the wooden staircase on the side of the clam bar.

"No, you come down."

"All right."

I told my friend what was going on. We both couldn't believe what was happening. It was a Jersey shore dream. Two girls wanted to drink beer with us. We quickly put on our jeans and washed our faces in the bathroom in the hall. I put the beer in a paper bag, and we flew down the wooden steps.

The girls were gone.

We started walking up the boardwalk. We both knew that we weren't cool enough to have a Jersey shore dream. We sat on a bench. We stared at the ocean. Our young souls had been so happy in those brief moments of putting on our jeans and washing our faces.

We'd been sitting there about five minutes when I happened to glance over my friend's shoulder and I saw the girls approaching us. The cuter of the two was carrying a little brown bag.

"We went to get a bottle of rum from my brother," she said. I was so happy that I probably had a growth spurt. I was only eighteen and didn't reach my full height until I was twenty.

The four of us went and hid under a pier and we drank our beer and rum. Eventually we paired off. I was better-looking than my friend, and I ended up with the very cute girl, who actually had the name of Rose. She had honey blond hair and she was waiflike, with delicate features and a rose of a mouth. She did have a strong Jersey accent, stronger than mine, but I didn't hold that against her.

My friend's girl had an all-right body, but she had bad teeth, which made her face sort of jowly, not pretty. My friend was pissed off that I got Rose, but I was lead dog in our little male pack of two, so I got the better girl.

Rose and I started making out and grinding into the wet sand. My friend put his arm around his girl, and the two of them stared at the surf.

When it was fully dark out, we all went up to the boardwalk and played some of the games in the stalls. We took secret sips from the rum, and Rose and I were holding hands. I felt on top of the world. I tried to win her a stuffed animal but failed.

When we were all bored with the games, I went to my car and got two blankets and I bought some more beer. We put the two blankets on the beach about twenty feet apart. Rose and I made out, and my friend and his girl sat on their blanket and didn't kiss. It was a little depressing to feel their gloom so nearby.

I said to Rose, "Do you want to go to my room?"

She did. I was having the best Jersey shore dream possible. We got to the room, and I kept the lights off so that she wouldn't see so clearly all the foot marks on the walls. There was a nice silvery light coming in the window from the boardwalk, and the footprints were obscured and looked perhaps like a wallpaper design.

The bed felt wonderful after being on the beach and we held one another and she was a gorgeous young girl. She was only sixteen, and her shirt came off and her erect nipples were like extra-long rubber pencil erasers. They stuck out at least an inch and a half from her tiny, nearly flat chest. I hadn't seen many nipples in my life, but I knew that these were unusual. (In fact, I've never seen nipples like that again.)

So it was a little freakish but also very inspiring. Her pants came off and there were no panties. It was the greatest night of my life. I lavished her whole body and the pencil erasers with kisses. In the nooks and crannies of her knees and elbows and in the sweet pucker of her belly button, I tasted Hawaiian Tropic suntan oil, and it was like an aphrodisiac.

"You can do it," she said.

*It.* I had done it with only two girls, and that had been after months of dating. And here above the boardwalk in Seaside Park, with the smell of frying clams in the air, a girl I had just met who had the longest nipples in the world was offering herself to me.

I kneeled above her and she opened her thin, smooth legs in a shy and endearing way. I peered down at her in the silvery light. I was nervous—I had made love maybe ten times in my life and had almost always experienced premature ejaculation—but I was also happy.

"Just pull out before . . . you know . . ." she said.

I lowered myself and I kissed her and I was about to enter her when there was a fierce banging on the door, and then I heard my friend say, "I'll go in." And then he was in the room, staring at me. I rose up and was kneeling between Rose's legs. Rose screamed and covered herself with the pillow.

"Oh, my God," my friend said. He was a virgin.

"GET THE HELL OUT OF HERE," I said. I've never been quick to anger, but this was one moment when I did feel rage, rather than depression, which is my usual response to conflict.

He backed out, a goofy smile on his face, and I felt sort of proud that he was really seeing what a lead dog I was. As soon as he closed the door, Rose's girlfriend with the funny jowls started screaming, "What's he doing in there? He's raping her."

Rose closed her legs and started crying.

No, I thought, this can't be. "We can still do it," I said to her.

The girlfriend was banging on the door. "Rose! Rose!"

"I'll be right out," Rose screamed through her tears.

"I'm coming in," said the girl, but there was some scuffling outside the door; my friend was obviously keeping the girl away from the door handle. I still had a chance. I was still maintaining my erection. Rose scooted to the end of the bed and started pulling on her pants.

"Let's do it really quick," I said. It was going to be quick anyway.

"No," she said angrily.

The halter top came on, the nipples were somehow pressed down, no one would suspect what odd treasures were hidden there.

"Are you all right, Rose?" the girlfriend called out.

"I'm all right," she answered.

She began to tie one of her sneakers, she was about to leave me, but I was still naked and still crazy with desire.

"Could you give me a blow job?" I asked in a sympathetic voice. I thought this was the kind of thing that a man might request under these circumstances. Also, I wanted to be able to report to my friend and to my friends back home that I had scored something significant on a dream of a Jersey shore night.

"Fuck you," she said, and she stood up and slapped me; it hardly caught my chin, and it didn't hurt.

"I'm sorry," I said. "I didn't think it was a bad thing to ask. I didn't mean to be rude. . . . Could I have your address? I'll write you."

She sat back down, and she tied her other sneaker. She stood up to leave.

"Please, could I have your address?"

She scrawled it on a piece of paper for me.

"I like you," I said. She didn't say anything back.

She left the room, and I wrapped a towel around my waist and sat on the bed. My friend, the idiot, came into the room.

"Why did you come back here?" I asked.

"That girl said she was going to go to the police if I didn't bring her here. We saw a cop on the boardwalk. She thought you were raping her."

We were silent. There were a few beers left. We started drinking them.

"Did you do it?" he asked.

"I was about to when you walked in. I was so close to having sex and you wrecked it."

He was happy. He was glad that I hadn't gotten laid. He didn't like being the number two dog. And in my own way I was sort of relieved. I knew I would have come in two seconds and disappointed her. I forgave my friend for coitus-interrupting-us.

We put our dirty feet up on the wall and rubbed them up and down. "Did you see her nipples?" I asked.

"No," he said. "I was looking at your ass. You looked really funny. Your ass is really white."

The next day we went home and I wrote Rose a long love letter. I apologized for how things had gone awry and for my horrible request of a blow job, without calling it a blow job. I wrote: "I'm sorry I asked for what I asked for."

I also proposed in the letter that we get together, that I come visit her.

But she never wrote me back.

So many a night for many years when I needed to come up with something, I would fantasize about completing what she and I had started that one summer night on the Jersey Shore. It was a potent image, and it never took me very long, about as long as it would have lasted then, and I would shudder and see photographs in my mind of those elongated nipples and the shy spreading of her legs.

# NOTES ON CAMDEN

## LAUREN GRODSTEIN

EXIT 4

1. The Adventure Aquarium in Camden, New Jersey, encourages its patrons to buy tickets in advance, and the tickets are expensive. I wonder: How many families in this city can afford nineteen dollars per person? Two thirds of Camden families live below the poverty line; the per capita income here is less than $10,000.

   But the aquarium is bright and clean and one of the loveliest public spaces in Camden: there are not only fish in residence but also sloths, toucans, hippopotami, and seals. I paid my nineteen dollars in advance; I walk right in.

2. In 2004, an organization called the Morgan Quitno Press named Camden, New Jersey, the most dangerous city in America.* In a country that boasts places like South Central Los Angeles and Detroit, Michigan, this is no minor distinction, but still the thing that strikes me most about Camden isn't the crime or the palpable fear. It's the emptiness. Entire neighborhoods seem drained of people. Houses have been boarded up; porches and roofs sag. The cars on the streets haven't been moved in months, and they are pocked with garbage and bird shit. There are no dry cleaners or movie theaters in evidence downtown, nor are there grocery stores. Driving through Camden, I have never felt nervous, but I have often felt heartbroken.

Yet there are bright spots in the city, and people who have known Camden for a long time swear that the place, for all its dreariness, is getting better. True, Camden is one of those places for which an upswing is always around the corner, since, for many residents, it can't get any worse. Nevertheless, the optimists have a point when they mention the new Tweeter Center,† where Coldplay and Eminem recently played sold-out concerts. The optimists win another point with the

---

* I, personally, had never heard of the Morgan Quitno Press before, but it seems to make a tiny splash every year with its bold-type rankings of comparative safety. For the record, in 2004 the safest American city was Newton, Massachusetts, which I had always thought of as a suburb.

† The Tweeter Center's Web site is careful not to mention Camden, New Jersey, too baldly. It labels itself "Tweeter Center at the Waterfront" and claims to serve Philadelphia and the South Jersey region.

Camden branch of Rutgers, the State University of New Jersey, with its genteel campus, its theater, gymnasium, and playing fields. I teach English and creative writing at Rutgers-Camden, and the students there are wonderful, an asset to any city. They are something to get excited about in Camden.

And there is other good news these days: a revitalized waterfront, a minor-league baseball team called the Riversharks, several handsome Federal buildings, and a beautiful neighborhood of row homes called Cooper Grant. A flourishing magnet school. A few local colleges. Brand-new loft apartments in the abandoned RCA Victor factory.

3. The RCA Victor factory, now abandoned, once brought hundreds of jobs to Camden.

The Haddon Craftsmen Printing Plant. Knox Gelatin. The Esterbrook Pen Company. The C. Howard Hunt Pen Company. The New York Shipbuilding Plant. Campbell's Soup. Gone, gone, almost entirely gone.

4. Under the dim lights of the aquarium, the hippopotamus is not aware of the urban blight scarring the city in which he resides. Of course, the hippopotamus is not a Camden native. He comes from Africa, which has its own problems: namely, for the hippo, drought, environmental degradation, and poaching. But here, in the cool confines of his West African River Experience diorama, the hippo dances dreamily. His West African River is glass-sided, and so we out in the audience can watch as

the hippo moves with surprising elegance in his gallons of brown water. He shakes and shimmies, waves his enormous ass at the crowd, brings his head above water and then slaps it back down, causing a terrific splash. The kids in the audience squeal and clap their hands; a young man keeps his video camera trained on the hippo's huge flanks. This hippo is a shameless flirt. I think, for a moment, he is winking at me.

5. I had my first interview for the Camden creative writing job the day before the *New York Times* published a very long and scary article entitled, cheekily, "Camden's Streets Go from Mean to Meanest." The reporter made Camden sound like a socialist Falluja, with "health benefits for drug dealers." He quoted the police chief: "I don't have enough soldiers. The enemy is out there. And we're fighting the same battle over and over and over again."

My mother called me the day the article came out. I was packing for my honeymoon (I'd gotten married three weeks before), trying to decide whether or not I had the chutzpah to actually wear the string bikini I'd bought for the occasion. It was past lunchtime, but I was too overwhelmed with work and luggage and exhaustion to eat. Still, I'd found a moment to read the *Times* that morning, and I'd been expecting one of my parents to call.

"You cannot take that job," said my mother, which is pretty much what I had expected her to say.

"Mom."

"I'm sorry, sweetheart. You cannot take this job. You just got married. You have your husband to think about."

"I have yet to even be offered the job, Mom. I'll worry about it when I get it. *If* I get it."

"You'll get the job, and then you'll get shot."

"I won't get shot."

"I'm not happy," my mother said.

Well, what mother in her right mind would be happy?

From the article in the *New York Times:* "In the past 12 months, there have been 53 homicides, including a 12-year-old shot to death on his porch for his radio, more than 800 aggravated assaults, including a toddler shot in the back of the head, at least 750 robberies and 150 acts of arson, more than 10,000 arrests and one glaring nonarrest—a serial rapist on the loose downtown."

Nobody, of course, had mentioned the rapist during my interview,* but even if they had it wouldn't have deterred me. The English Department at Rutgers is wonderful, and I wanted the job.

6. I grew up in New Jersey, but in the northeast corner of the state, a few miles south of the New York border. The town was called Haworth; it had been named for Haworth, England, which is where the Brontë sisters

---

* The rapist was dispatched several months later by a local resident; the entire city let out its breath.

grew up. A postcard of the English Haworth hangs in the post office, and I imagine that more than one citizen of Haworth, New Jersey, has made the pilgrimage to the town's English counterpart to marvel at the sheep pastures there and note that while New Jersey's Haworth has three beauty salons and two Italian restaurants, the English version has neither one nor the other.

When I was a child in Haworth, New Jersey, my universe was made up of the Haworth School (K–8), Haworth Pizza, the Haworth Library, and Manhattan, a thirty-minute commute without traffic. It never occurred to me—why should it have occurred to me?— that New Jersey was more than the Palisades Parkway to the Upper West Side, liquor runs to Washington Heights, and baseball games at Shea Stadium. As far as I could tell, New Jersey as a state didn't seem to have much to say for itself; it existed solely for people who wanted to live in New York or Philadelphia but also wanted their kids to have backyards.

I did not know that there were places in New Jersey where people died at twice the rate they did in the rest of the country, where unemployment was more than three times the national average. It never occurred to me that there were places in New Jersey where many babies did not survive their first year.

7. When I was just out of college I worked at a women's health consortium and met a nurse from Trenton. We were talking about vacations one day—it was summer, after all—and I told her that whenever I went on vaca-

tion I liked to visit the local aquarium. I have many reasons for loving aquariums: they are dark and cool, calming on a family vacation, and the fish are so beautiful (or bulgy-headed or grumpy-looking). Sometimes they'll swim up and kiss you through the glass of their tanks. I told the nurse about visiting the aquariums in Baltimore, San Diego, and Mystic, Connecticut; I told her that my favorite was the aquarium in Monterey, since it had that incredible otter exhibit and the giant octopus.

"How about New Jersey?" the nurse said. "What do you think of Camden's aquarium?"

I looked at her blankly. I had never heard of Camden.

"Really?" the nurse said, both surprised and disappointed. "This is your own state," she said. "You grew up here, right? How could you not know where you come from?"

8. So now I'm getting to know Camden. I work here, I write here, I sit outside here when the weather is warm, drinking coffee from the campus Starbucks. I've learned to feel safe enough in this city to pause on the sidewalk and admire the vestigial architecture; it doesn't take much imagination to see how beautiful these neighborhoods would be if people started moving back and fixing them up. Were Camden a neighborhood in New York City, it would be gentrifying giddily. Some developer would pay for the environmental clean-up on the waterfront, and new bistros and shoe

stores would be sprouting like mushrooms. That shell on the corner, that boarded-up three story with the Federal details? You wouldn't be able to afford it.

Any New Yorker who visits Camden can't help but think of gentrification, of available square footage, of possibility. And as I write, there are local groups working feverishly to improve Camden's environment, employment opportunities, housing. There is hope here. But as I'm staring at the shell of the hotel, two stray dogs run down the street, barking madly, and I keep walking.

9. At the Adventure Aquarium, there's a shallow tank filled with southern stingrays and smooth dogfish sharks.* The stingrays and sharks are there to be touched—there's a guide showing us how to do it— but still it feels incredibly transgressive to attempt to pet one of these things. A child across the tank starts to cry; another one starts to giggle hysterically. A lady standing next to me has her arm all the way in, up almost to her armpit, and her eyes are closed. She's humming as she reaches for the animals.

A stingray's wings feel gelatinous and cold, like face cream that's been in the refrigerator for a while. The wings flap gently back and forth as the stingrays swim

---

* I know it sounds crazy to have an open shark tank in a public place full of kids, but actually the dogfish shark isn't a big biter—it uses its teeth to grind—and anyway, these particular sharks seem sluggish and stupid, as if they don't even realize they're being touched.

under our curious fingers. They look like angels, and after a few minutes watching them, I get the feeling that, if a stingray could stand up, it might wrap its wings around me and give me a hug. I get the feeling that if a stingray stung me it would feel really sorry about it afterward. I get the feeling that the stingray wishes it never had to use that stinger at all. A stingray dawdles under my hand. I stroke its wing gently before it darts away, relishing that jellylike coolness on my fingertips. This is possibly the most dangerous thing I have done since I've arrived in Camden.* Still, I feel completely safe. The stingray won't bite me—I can just tell.

It occurs to me again how much I like it here.

Outside, the rain begins to pound, but I forgot my umbrella, so I head to the gift shop to buy one. I expect aquarium umbrellas to be adorned with schools of fish or maybe bright plastic tentacles, but instead they're sedate and compact, navy blue with the words "Adventure Aquarium" written on one side. They cost eight dollars.

"Is it raining in Philadelphia?" the salesgirl asks as she rings me up.

"Excuse me?"

"You came from Philadelphia, right?" Well, yes, Philadelphia's where a lot of the Rutgers faculty live; it's just across the river from Camden.

---

* Sure, the ray has been neutered, but still the animal has a jagged, serrated spine, a knifelike tail, and nowhere to hide.

"I was in Philadelphia this morning," I say, and then add, "it wasn't raining then."

"I'm not surprised," the salesgirl said. "Sometimes you don't even get a cloud in Philadelphia, but it rains buckets here in Camden. I don't know why."

"Strange."

"Always raining," the girl says blankly, handing me my change.

I don't know what to say to her. I take my umbrella and head out into the silent streets, the sad, beautiful buildings, the deluge.

# A RUMBLE AND A SCREAM

## CAREN LISSNER

EXIT 7A

I sat in the back seat of my car on many hot nights that summer, watching heat lightning flash silently across the sky and wondering how—in the span of a few weeks—I had gone from Ivy League college freshman to homeless amusement park worker.

Each day, I lingered at my job at Six Flags Great Adventure as late as possible, hoping for favorable weather so the managers wouldn't send us home early. After my shift ended, I repaired to the locker room, changed out of my tight green-and-white uniform, and washed off the day's sweat in the shower. Then I aimed my used Plymouth Duster at hotels in

Freehold, Princeton, or anywhere else nearby that had a dark parking lot where I could motor in, cut the lights, and snooze in the backseat until sunup. While the Town House Motel near Princeton afforded access to a rumbling ice machine on the second floor, the Sheraton on Route 537 boasted a larger parking lot that would shield me from discovery.

My parents were fighting over the terms of their divorce that summer, and it wasn't comfortable to live with either of them. My mother had just left our native Central Jersey to search for a cheap apartment in upstate New York, and she was moving from motel to motel. Even if she had had a stable place to live, there weren't many summer jobs up there. But she convinced me that if I lived full-time with my father in New Jersey and not with her, he would be exempt from paying my college tuition. It also became clear that to live with one parent would be a slight to the other. It seemed best to avoid both of them, find a job in a place I knew, and sleep in my car near work. Both of them complained about not having enough money, so I couldn't ask for any. In retrospect, perhaps, I could have done things differently, but I was only nineteen.

Great Adventure was a known entity. It was five miles from farmy, colonial Freehold, the suburban Central Jersey town where I'd grown up; it paid more than minimum wage; and it employed 3,200 seasonal workers each summer. There had to be a place there for me.

In the past, I had never seen the country's largest theme park as a source of sustenance. It was where twelfth-graders sneaked for "Senior Cut Day"; where bubble blowers contributed to a piece of unsanctioned, unsavory art known as the "Gum Wall" (so famous was its sordid legend that my fourth-grade teacher once commented in class on how disgusting it was), and where any New Jerseyan under sixteen who wanted to prove himself cool would acquire a season pass and boast of multiple rides on Lightnin' Loops. For a younger version of me, the park had clutched freedom and wonder in its tiger claws, promising three-scoop sundaes at Yum Yum Palace and a refreshing splash on the Log Flume.

I took the swing shift at Great Adventure, from noon to 8 P.M. I needed the $4.75 per hour to cover car insurance, gas, and food for three months before I could return to college in Philadelphia for sophomore year. If I could survive and get back to my dorm room and my new friends—who, I imagined, were having much different summers than I was—I'd be okay.

My job was at the park's entrance, among the long row of admissions turnstiles. Visitors would hand me their ticket, pass through the turnstile, stroll through the metal detector, and have their purse carefully probed for contraband by a Great Adventure security guard. Then they'd plunge into the delightful aromas of fried dough and powdered sugar.

My coworkers included retirees from the numerous fifty-five-and-over retirement communities that were (and still are) burgeoning in Central Jersey, as well as college students like me who were home in the 'burbs for the summer. I envied the other ticket takers, as they often seemed happy to get sent home early on slow days, even if it meant lost wages. Their paychecks went to extraneous pursuits like travel and movies, but mine were used for gas and car repairs. Whenever Eddie the Evil Manager came out of his booth and fixed us with his coal-eyed stare, figuring out whom to send home next, I always ducked behind the metal detectors, hoping it wouldn't be me.

Leaving the park each evening at twilight, I purposely avoided the main highway, Route 195, which runs horizontally from Trenton to the shore, cutting the state in two. I couldn't bear to be among the suited commuters rushing home. Great Adventure was only ten minutes from the hotels, and I thought that driving slowly on back roads would save me gas. I crept north along the thinnest, spookiest, and most poorly lit thoroughfares possible. Central Jersey was the location of the Battle of Monmouth and various other Revolutionary War sites, and is riddled with ancient horse farms, dilapidated eighteenth-century shacks, and streets still named for structures that haven't existed in a hundred years. I took Carrs Tavern Road (though I couldn't find the tavern), Millstone Road (the mill must have been around there somewhere), and Stagecoach Road—the former route of the Philly–to–Long Branch stage. Surrounded by hayfields and darkness, I would climb an incline at fifteen miles per hour, lift my foot off the pedal, and coast downward among sloping hills where I could smell mud and horse droppings.

Great Adventure's 2,200 acres are situated in the otherwise unremarkable Central Jersey town of Jackson. The location was chosen in the 1970s because it was roughly equidistant from New York (seventy miles) and Philadelphia (fifty-two), and smack in the middle of nowhere. If you head just ten miles north, you are within an hour of Manhattan. But being the slightest sliver south of commuting distance is all it takes to keep a New Jersey town in anonymity. Freehold Township, where I grew up, is slightly northeast of Jackson and thus slightly more expensive, with better schools.

On my fourth day working at the park, I met Owen.

Owen instantly seemed different from everyone else. He had shiny black hair from his unique Indian/Israeli heritage, little round glasses, a 3.4 average at Princeton, and a wry, subversive style of humor.

I would have expected his nascent Princeton education to have propelled him into an internship at NBC or the David Sarnoff Research Center, but instead, he was at the amusement park like me. And also like me, he wanted to be a writer someday. In his free time, he worked on a summer project that seemed to me to be far from pretentious: a humorous novel about coming of age in the '80s. It was exactly the kind of thing I wanted to write. At school he was majoring in English and Eastern religion.

Coming into work each morning, I wished fervently that the manager would station Owen and me side by side, so we could talk all day. I loved his running commentary. Like any good writer, Owen noticed *everything*.

"That girl's hair was *this* high!" he said to me one day, as a gum-snapping Jersey Girl passed through the gate.

"People say the same stupid thing when they go through the metal detectors," he observed, groaning. "'Oh, I better put my Uzi away.'"

I chimed in: "Or 'I've got a metal plate in my head.'"

"Yeah, that's a good one. Or 'I left my grenade in my other pants.'"

"'My bomb is back in the car.'"

Back then, terrorism jokes were actually funny.


Watching people go through the metal detectors was actually the sport of choice for us admissions workers. The security guards with their probing sticks took many guests by surprise, even though a sign warned each entrant that the park was private property and they would be subject to a search. No fanny pack was left unprobed. A female security guard told me that one time, they caught a mother with cocaine, and they had to detain her for the Jackson police while her young daughter sat crying in the office. Other times, patrons would step through the turnstiles, suddenly notice the line of guards, and race back out to the parking lot. Items confiscated while I worked there included marijuana, pocketknives, and illegal three-finger rings.

One drizzly afternoon, I was blissfully working alongside Owen, hoping I could somehow get him to like me, and a tall Rastafarian man approached our gates. Owen and I noticed him at the same time.

The guy suddenly realized the security guards were behind us and mumbled in a baritone, "There's some shit I gotta get rid of." Then he backtracked to a garbage pail near the bushes and tossed something in.

After he was gone, Owen volunteered to go check what was in the trash.

Owen returned to me with his hands spread five feet apart. "A huuuuuge condom," he said. "Used."


I thought about Owen at night when I lay across the backseat in the Sheraton parking lot, trees shielding me from the lights. I could hear car doors slamming and weary families getting out. My saving grace was music. I would put on my Walkman headphones, close my eyes, and listen to cassettes of the 1970s and 1980s pop groups I'd grown up with. My tabletop stereo, the one that had gotten me through high school and my freshman year of college, was stored away in the trunk of the car, but at least I had my Walkman. As I listened to the songs, I thought of living on my own someday and not depending on anyone for anything.

Occasionally, if it was a brutally hot night, I would head into the hotel for ice and rub it along the back of my neck.

Sometimes I tried to guess what Owen was doing at the same time. He lived in wealthy West Windsor with his older brother and parents. I figured he was up on his windowsill writing among the eaves, inhaling the cut grass and trying to select a fresh metaphor to describe the garden hose. Was it possible he could ever like me? I was probably far too nervous around him (and all boys) to hope for that. I certainly hadn't told Owen of my housing situation—and I didn't know if I should.

•　•　•

During the second week of work, I decided to drive to the middle-class house in Freehold where I'd lived before my family's downward tumble.

It was a three-bedroom Levitt home with cathedral ceilings on an eighth of an acre, part of a spacious 1970s development called "Contempra at Monmouth Heights" near Route 9. We had a wide, flat front yard that became the de facto site for after-school kickball games. Even the bullies who taunted my little brother at school and the popular girls who turned up their noses at me in junior high participated in a temporary truce during the games, since the social order was different at home than at school. I was one of the older kids on my block and thus had more confidence, so I could boot a kickball clear into the next yard. At school, I was less athletic and was among the last picked in gym. It was amazing how much my abilities improved during the ten minutes I rode the bus home.

Although some people denigrate the suburbs, I thrived there. I biked around pretending to be Harriet the Spy; my brother and I rolled up our pants and inched along the stream at the end of the road, hunting for geodes and frogs. Every street in our development was named for a Revolutionary War site or figure (Ticonderoga Boulevard, Gage Court), and it was there that my brother and I prowled at twilight, mapping our own "battle routes" for Halloween in order to maximize treat intake. Pillowcases were filled to the hilt with Dum Dum Pops and KitKats.

Alongside the local stream, which was actually a waning tributary of the Manasquan River, lay a tiny "pocket park" with a small wooden pavilion and jungle gym. There, kids staged fights, made out, and coated the pavilion with spray-painted graffiti. There were laconic reviews of Van Halen ("VH #1!!!"), sincere declarations of fidelity ("TL + LF = TLF!"), and evidence that the famous bard of the bathrooms hadn't missed our gentle hamlet: "Here I sit / broken hearted / come to shit / but only farted."

The first time I noticed that quatrain, I was ten years old and found it terrifically profound. When I returned many years later, I was comforted that the wise words were still there.


I got to know other people at Great Adventure besides Owen, although I didn't know if I could confide in them or hang out with them after work. Moe, a twenty-five-year-old apple-cheeked security guard with a buzz cut, kept asking me to see a movie with him. Moe asked every girl out. He was also separated from his third wife, who lived in California.

"So," he said to me the day he met me, raising and lowering his eyebrows, "are you?"

"Am I what?"

"Just are you?"

"Am I what?"

"Just answer yes or no."

"Okay. Yes, I am."

"Ha!" He said. "Ha ha! It was 'Are you a virgin?' Ha ha ha ha!"

Then he walked away.

A few days later, he told me, "You're cute, Caren. Don't let anyone tell you otherwise."

When he asked me to the movies, I imagined relaxing in the air-conditioned Amboy Multiplex on Route 35 instead of staring up at the glowing SHERATON sign at night. Then, I imagined Moe beside me in a dark theater. At nineteen, my dating experience had been limited to walks across campus with a curly-haired kid whom I'd met in a prefreshman honors program. I didn't know if a fellow of Moe's experience would be the right introduction to male/female relations.

I declined the opportunity, although I wasn't even experienced enough to know how to say "no" properly. I nervously mumbled, "I can't get into anything right now."

"Don't get me wrong," he said. "I'm not asking for a relationship. I just want a date. Fuck; I'm married."


There was still Owen. Owen was smart. Owen was funny. Owen never spoke of having a girlfriend or "crazy" ex.

But Owen didn't show up for staff events after work, like employee Bingo, where you could win a giant teddy bear. Owen was always the first one to volunteer to go home on a soggy day, deserting me for grass and books.

I wished for another coworker to connect with. My prospects were few. There were Irene, a red-haired senior citizen who believed people were stealing from her locker, and Jeremy, the kid with the glass eye, who constantly taunted Pryce, the gay kid. (Apparently, cyclopes ranked higher in the pecking order than homosexuals.) There was Traci, a gossip-monger who wanted to know which one of us was really working in "IV" (Investigations). IV was a specially trained undercover Great Adventure unit that tried to catch employees violating company policy. IV really existed, and we never did find out who among us was a spy.

As time went on, I found new ways to linger at the park before leaving. In the locker room, I stuffed ideas into the employee suggestion box: "Don't let the managers send admissions workers home early." "Serve funnel cake in the employee cafeteria." One day I scribbled a suggestion asking if there were health effects from standing near the metal detectors all summer.

I stuffed all my suggestions into the box and temporarily forgot about them.

I did find something to look forward to at Great Adventure one Friday night. They were planning a concert at the North Star Arena that would feature a few of the '70s bands I listened to on my Walkman. The show was called "Legends of Rock and Roll" and would be hosted by a DJ from New Jersey 101.5 who was trying to oust Governor Jim Florio with his "Hands Across New Jersey" tax protest. I didn't care about the DJ or taxes, but I was excited that one of the singers from Three Dog Night would be there. I'd been listening to that goofy '70s band a lot lately, particularly a song called "Out in the Country" that made me feel hopeful about being free.

The night of the concert, Eddie the Evil Manager walked toward our gates to send some of us home early. This was one time I didn't mind.

I trundled through the land of damp concrete and cotton candy to the back fence of the North Star Arena. I convinced a security guard to hand my Three Dog Night tape to Chuck Negron for an autograph. It worked, and I was thrilled.

Meanwhile, I was learning to pinch pennies to a degree I'd never known. I craved the crisp funnel cakes whose fumes I inhaled at work all day, but I never let myself squander four bucks on them. I might need that money for emergency car repairs. Often my mother asked me to drive up to upstate New York on my days off to help her look for a place to live, which meant extra gas and tolls. On some nights I stayed in my father's basement.

One afternoon, a woman accidentally dropped a dollar on the ground as she approached my gate. She didn't notice it, and I stared at it intently. It curled and beckoned like a tasty fish. Normally I would have returned the wrinkled greenback right away, but this time I just eyed it.

Then the woman realized it was there and snatched it.

Midway through the summer, Ali and Tim came into the park.

Ali and Tim were friends from my freshman dorm in Philadelphia. There's nothing that bonds a bunch of eighteen-year-olds like being confused and away from home for the first time. Tim was from a well-off family in Alaska and had informed us the first day of school that "No, I don't live in an igloo, no, my parents aren't Eskimos, and yes, we do speak English there." Ali was a midyear transfer student from Maryland. They were visiting the area and had heard that I worked at the park. So they had called me the day before in the park office, and I told them I could give them guest passes.

"Hey," Ali said, slapping me five as he came through my gate. "Thanks for the passes."

"No problem," I said. Then I added half jokingly, "Just get me a funnel cake before you leave."

Behind me, the line for funnel cakes wound around a building.

I added hopefully, "I can't afford one."

"Very funny," Ali said.

"Yeah," Tim said. "See you later."

I continued to passively-aggressively make inroads with Owen. In our orange plastic ponchos in the rain, we kidded about the metal detectors, talked books, and imitated tourists from Boston ("What time does the safehhhri pahhhk close?"). One warm night, as the sun dodged clouds tinged with pink, we talked about our all-time favorite movies. I tried to steer our discussion toward current films we wanted to see—*Dick Tracy? Total Recall? Ghost?*—so he might suggest seeing one after work. After all, if Moe could suggest that, why couldn't someone like Owen?

Right as we were broaching current flicks, Eddie the Evil Manager approached us.

"We're a little overstaffed today," Eddie said. "We need three people to sign out early."

Owen raised his hand. I watched him disappear toward the locker room.

The weather got hotter and hotter, and they hired more staff to deal with daytime crowds. One of the new guys, Adrian, might have competed with Owen for admissions gate heart-throb. He was a musician with delightfully scrumptious stubble. Unfortunately, he was dumb as rocks. As a result, Eddie the Evil Manager stuck him at the hand stamp entrance, where all he had to do was watch people shove their branded paws under the black light. His other main task was to keep guests from accidentally leaving the park through that particular gate, but he couldn't even get that right. His method was to stand in front of them, spread his arms, and intone, "This is not an exit." He never pointed to the *correct* exit, just became a human shield, repeating the same phrase over and over until I was ready to throttle him.

The park got busier as August clambered on. Happy families bounced through the turnstiles to munch funnel cake and get their pictures taken with Bugs Bunny.

The second week in August, Eddie the Evil Manager came toward my gate, but this time, it was not to send me home early.

"Joe Lawson is on the phone for you," he said, his eyes wide. Everyone stared at me.

We all knew who Joe Lawson was. He was the vice president of the entire park. What did he want?

I traveled forward to the main booth, followed by many pairs of eyes.

Then Eddie shut the door, and I was on the phone alone.

"I just wanted to let you know that we got your suggestion about the metal detectors," Joe Lawson said.

I looked around the booth, at the cash register, the pile of Coke coupons.

"We're going to do some research and get back to you in a couple of weeks," Joe added.

"Thanks," I said. "Thank you."

Then I hung up.

I knew that I would probably be back in Philadelphia before he could respond to me, but it didn't matter. The important thing was that I had gotten a call from Joe Lawson and my coworkers knew it.

When I walked back to the admissions gate, they watched me with fear and respect. No one dared ask what Joe had wanted.

Even if I was stuck between both of my parents that summer, even if I was stuck between homes, and even if I was stuck smack in the center of Jersey between New York and Philadelphia, in that moment, when everyone wondered what had transpired between me and my boss's boss's boss, I was the one with power.

Eddie never sent me home early after that. I didn't know if it was because of the heat or because I had associated with Joe, but I didn't care. I was just happy to be earning extra dough.


The last week in August, I sat in front of the giant fountain and let the sprinkles of water cool my neck. I filled my lungs with sweet air; I listened to the sound of the roller coasters—first a rumble, then a scream.

I completed my application for sophomore move-in at college. I would be living in a room that was big and boxy, with a view of the Philadelphia skyline and the electronic messages scrolling across the Philadelphia Electric Company building.

Owen had already left with barely a good-bye. Moe the security guard was long gone, back to California to figure things out with his wife. Mostly there remained senior citizens from the early-retirement communities—Rossmoor, Clearbrook.

But there was still Adrian, still manning the hand stamp entrance with his special finesse. Before the park closed on my last night there, before the Friday-night fireworks burst over the lake, a burly woman stomped toward him. Adrian faced her, pressed his beefy paws against the rails, and stared her down.

"This is not an exit," Adrian said.

Maybe not, I thought, but tonight, it will be for me.

# SUBURBAN LEGENDS

### ELIZABETH KEENAN

EXIT 9

**W**hen I was young, I had a preoccupation with the scary and unexplainable. The mysterious side of things invigorated me in the same way the roller coasters at Great Adventure did for my friends. Scary movies, Stephen King novels, and campfire ghost stories were happiness. My fascination with the strange side of the Garden State began the first day my family moved to Princeton Junction and I met a girl exactly my age, with the same name—Elizabeth—and freckles like mine, living across the street. We were similar in every way and were best friends immediately. We fancied ourselves doppelgängers similar to the twins in

*The Shining*—a movie that scared us thoroughly no matter how many times we watched it. And in an act of ultimate solidarity, we sealed our friendship with pinpricked fingers on the sidewalk in front of our houses, blood sisters forever.

Throughout high school our exposure to actual death was limited to the multiple fatalities that occurred in our town year after year on the periphery of our self-absorbed teen lives. We'd never personally known anyone who died, so mortality was no more within our realm of understanding than giving birth. The morning announcements by our solemn principal breaking the news "that another terrible tragedy has struck our town" became almost too frequent to be truly absorbed. In the same way that the evening news became a murmur in the background of our lives (tuned out by marathon three-way phone conversations), our town's suicides, murders, and fatal car accidents were tragedies happening to other people, never to us.

From the beginning of our ghost chasing, the neighborhood was Liz's and my world to explore, and our fascination with ghostly places began when we heard that the woods behind the Little League field were haunted. Peculiar events always happened in the woods, according to a classmate who lived near them. We went exploring armed with a Ouija board and active imaginations. According to Milton Bradley's plastic planchette, the woods were haunted by an unhappy widower who was angry his house had been destroyed and his baby taken from him. Shortly after making contact with our ghost, we came upon a half-buried shack and a burned black-and-white photo of a man and a baby. We freaked and hightailed it out of the woods. But we believed, and we were *hooked*.

As we got older, we learned through stories told on back-yard camping trips and from friends' older siblings that our state was a veritable amusement park ride of horrors, with each exit offering its own pocket of scary. Our own Mercer County was a hotbed of creepy places in spite of its endless sea of cookie-cutter McMansions and its outwardly polished appearance.

There was a spot in the elementary school playground near our neighborhood where we heard a senior had killed himself on the middle swing. Allegedly he haunted the place nightly, his spirit bound to the rusty old swing set forever. After midnight, when the streetlights switched off, we'd signal with flashlights from our respective windows, our similar split ranch houses facing each other from either side of the street. We had a code: two flickers to confirm our parents were asleep and the green light for our witching hour, three flickers if we were stuck in the house and couldn't sneak out. The excitement and anticipation of the returned light in the pitch blackness set the perfect spooky ambience.

Once the coast was clear, Liz and I would sneak out and meet in the middle of the street, revved with the adrenaline of being free to roam and explore in the quiet of the late hours. We'd sit on either side of the "death" swing, dragging our Keds across the sand and gravel, talking about why these ghosts were caught in eternal limbo, destined to haunt the same spot every night. While waiting to see the ghost swinging beside us, we scared ourselves and each other by pondering where we would haunt if we were stuck between the living and the dead. We never saw the boy, but the creaking of the old chains in the dead of the night made us shiver with possibility.

Supposedly the annual haunted hayride in Toms River was really haunted by the kid who accidentally hanged himself while setting up his post as the "hanged man." He miscalculated his noose and died instantly, hanging undiscovered for an entire night while kids rolled by in hay-filled flatbeds, wide-eyed and laughing over the realistic corpse. Liz made me go on the hayride three times, convinced that we would see his ghost if the timing was right. We never saw him, and while I was secretly relieved, she was interminably unafraid and frustrated by our fruitless rides.

Liz's fearlessness marked the major difference between us. She was the first one to enter abandoned dwellings or walk through a cemetery alone; I was the opposite, with one foot out the door, always ready to run if necessary. She also pioneered pot smoking and drinking, while I stayed in the shadows, my foot always poised to run, as afraid of these new factors as I was of the deserted houses and quiet roads. While I tried to keep up, I remained the fearful half, and by twelfth grade there were places she was going that I just could not follow.

Back in tenth grade we were testing our limits daily, flirting with the unseen as much as the boys in our classes. We told third-person accounts of ghost sightings at peer counseling retreats, sleepovers, and cast parties. Stories of a girl dressed in white who had been run down on her prom night and wandered the same stretch of road night after night inspired us to visit the site of her death. An abandoned haunted farmhouse behind an old gas station begged for a videotaped walk-through without a flashlight. We'd ride our bikes to the far reaches of our neighborhood and walk along the old railroad tracks, trying to spot the "floating" lady another friend claimed to have witnessed one night.

Some of us even lived in the haunted places. A friend lived in the house Orson Welles had stayed in when he performed his infamous "War of the Worlds" broadcast on Halloween in 1938. She claimed the house was ripe with weird noises and doors slamming in the night. We listened to the radio recording in our fifth-grade class one Halloween, lying in the dark under our desks, enchanted by Welles's dynamic voice, imagining the residents of New Jersey panicking and evacuating, unaware that the "news" broadcast of an alien invasion in their very own Grover's Mill was fictional. Spending a night in the house overlooking the mill and park where the alien landing had supposedly occurred was unparalleled. We stayed up all night waiting for a confirmation of anything paranormal or even extraterrestrial. It was our first high, and, for Liz especially, the rush was addictive.

Favorite haunted spots included the movie theater in Atco Township, where invisible hands were reported to move across your neck and shoulders in the dark. Gravity Hill on Route 208 was an especially notorious place. By many accounts, if you parked your car in neutral at the bottom of a hill at a particular intersection, the ghost of a woman who'd been hit in that very spot would push you up the hill, away from danger. People had supposedly peppered their trunks with flour and found handprints afterward (we could never actually find the spot). There was a famous hotel in Howell where the press had camped out in the 1930s when the Lindbergh baby was kidnapped and murdered and a road in northern New Jersey, built over the grave site of thirteen executed witches, with thirteen bumps that kept emerging no matter how many times they repaved the road flat.

We never saw actual ghosts when we went hunting for haunted spots, but someone would always claim they saw a shadow or figure in the dark. The bravest people, always led by Liz, would go into deserted houses alone or walk alone in the cornfields behind the Market Fair mall off Route 1. Sometimes we encountered entities far scarier than ghosts. Freshman year, a story of a house with a pitchfork-wielding ghost caused a carload of us to seek proof. We rolled up a long driveway leading to a seemingly deserted farmhouse and flicked the high beams three times, as we had been instructed, waiting with racing hearts. Sure enough, a figure emerged from the house, armed not with a pitchfork but with a rifle. We quickly realized he wasn't a ghost but the owner of the house, who was livid about the carloads of kids trespassing on his land every night.

Getting our driver's licenses junior year changed our haunted outings forever. Catapulting us out of the confines of our limited town, the entire state and all of its boogeymen were ours to discover (and the gas was cheap). Every weekend Liz and I drove around in my beat-up Honda, drifting into undiscovered towns, eager for new undiscovered stories. We soon learned that all roads in our state eventually led home if we drove long enough.

In Cranbury, we'd park near the haunted inn on Main Street late at night to watch the shadows move across the front lawn or drive slowly through the expansive cemetery with the headlights turned off. I was always too scared to get out of the car, but Liz got out alone and sat atop a headstone in the pitch blackness for five minutes. I watched her from the car, a dark shape on a granite headstone in the moonlight. That sight of her was more eerie than any of our supposed ghosts. This would be a haunting memory of Liz for me when her ashes were buried in the same cemetery by year's end.

The searches for the haunted places allowed us to transcend our narrow lives and identify with something unseen. Being a teenager was not unlike being a ghost, an unsettled spirit stuck between two worlds. We'd wax philosophical on life and death and what we thought we were going to do once we got out of our town—*if* we got out alive, considering all the people who hadn't. Nobody cool ever lived to see Social Security.

Death in many ways was the sexier option, as seen on TV and in the lyrics and words of our idols; Morrison, Cobain, and Plath, Joplin, Woolf, and Kerouac, to name a few. And as we moved closer to the big unknown—graduation, college, *real life*—Liz began to tempt fate with drinking and hard drugs, both of which mixed badly with her insatiable fearlessness. One high was never enough; there was always something more intoxicating to explore. While she edged closer to dangerous places, I resolved to live long enough to see what was beyond our state's borders.

It wasn't just us. Everywhere I went in the state, I met ghost- and boogeymen-obsessed teenagers like us. And everyone had a story that was truer or scarier than ours. So what was the fascination? Why was New Jersey the nucleus of creepy? One would think Massachusetts would be the more likely state for the paranormal, with the Salem Witch Trials and the eighty-six-year curse on the Red Sox. Or Maine, whose spooky history came from the typewriter of Stephen King. Something about New Jersey draws this peculiar side out of everybody; maybe it is something in the water.

I blame it on the New Jersey Devil.

Jerseyans love their Devil. I have to question a state that made something that terrorized residents for more than three hundred years into a lovable hockey team mascot. The first legend we had all heard was about the Devil. Everyone we knew had an ancestor who had been alive during the Jersey Devil's reign of terror in the Pine Barrens and claimed to have seen it firsthand.

The Jersey Devil wasn't a ghost, at least not originally. According to legend, the Devil was a mythical creature that had been terrorizing and killing around coastal New Jersey since the 1700s. The Jersey Devil was the original myth of the state.

The birthplace of the Jersey Devil was the elusive Pine Barrens, the Everest of scary places in the state. Supposedly the woods are almost as expansive as Yellowstone and deadly because of not only their resident demon but their denseness, for anyone who wanders in sans compass. The origin myth of the Devil varied depending on who was telling it. The amalgamated version that I remember is that there was a woman named Leeds who lived in the Pine Barrens in the 1800s. She was poor, alone, and taking care of a dozen kids. The father of the children varied, from the local clergyman making sinful visits to Ms. Leeds or the Devil himself posing as a male suitor. Another version is that the town cursed Ms. Leeds for being a floozy, probably a variation on Hester Prynne from high school English class.

Leeds was the first of many single mothers in New Jersey trying to make ends meet without any help from the babies' daddy or state assistance. She got pregnant with another child—unlucky thirteenth—and cursed God, convinced that this one was sure to be the Devil, understandably. The thirteenth spawn was a hybrid creature with a horse's head, a snake's body, bat's wings, and goat's hooves. Born to a terrified mother and siblings, it quickly maimed and killed the whole family. It then went on to terrorize and kill anyone who came into the Pine Barrens and had the unfortunate luck of crossing its path.

Nobody could kill it, but according to legend, people tried, including Napoleon's brother and Commodore Stephen Decatur, who shot a cannonball at the Devil that went right through it. Some people maintained that the Jersey Devil was immortal and still roamed the woods in all of its Frankenanimal glory (there are published reports of sightings and attacks up until 1987). Others claimed that the original Jersey Devil was long dead and the Barrens were haunted not by the Devil but by the spirits of all its victims.

By junior year, I wanted to get out of New Jersey more than ever and was counting down the days until graduation. Finally, I would be done with the mall, diner food, and the endless drama that went along with being a teenager. While I was stressing about getting into college, Liz was graduating from hard alcohol to cocaine. The more certain I became about wanting to survive high school, the more things were spinning out of control for her: a trip to rehab, a car accident, numerous tattoos. During her weekly Al-Anon meetings, Liz would find a place to sleep while I would sob over the collective stories of lives ruined by drugs. Often I felt that I was incapable of being a friend to her, but I couldn't let go completely. I would always be the scared girl ready to run, while she was still miles ahead of me, testing the limits of her seemingly immortal teenage self.

By senior year, the haunted-spot drive-bys had all but lost their novelty. We had more interesting things to do, like play quarters and flip-cup in the houses of friends whose parents were out of town and hang out at Hoagie Haven in Princeton, than drive around aimlessly. Liz and I had stopped hanging out but still saw each other leaving for school every morning and in the hallways, familiar strangers in the sea of our peers. The urge to reach out to her still remained, but I fought it, scared to get pulled in again.

One night, while I was sitting on my front stoop, I spotted Liz hanging by her mailbox, basking in the warmth of new spring. We waved at each other as timidly as we had the first day I'd moved in. We moved toward each other, barefoot in the middle of the street. She looked composed and sober, and we talked and laughed about the loss of time and the way our lives had changed.

We giggled about the upcoming senior class trip and prom, surprisingly two events that she was looking forward to in spite of her aversion to school events. Liz shrugged off her bad run, making it hard to remember what had really driven us apart while she talked about her plans for community college and her new passion for photography. Her lucidity and excitement filled me with hope. We reminisced about all of our adventures chasing ghosts and our collective disappointment in never having seen an actual apparition. In a gesture of solidarity and tribute to our receding childhood, we made a pact to go on one last ride together, to find the Jersey Devil.

The night we drove to the Pine Barrens, we found it by accident. We knew a general direction and exit number, and drove until there were no more 7-Elevens. We were told by an amused Mobil attendant to take Exit 48 and find Moss Mill Road and we would find Leeds Point. There is *nothing* going on in that part of New Jersey aside from pine trees. In fact, it is one of the few places that have remained untainted by the rampant housing developers. It is also one of the scariest places I've been in. We finally found *the* road, Scott's Hill Landing, that we had read about in so many stories about the Jersey Devil, and we shrieked triumphantly upon finding it as we rode it to where the pavement turned to sand. The road was sandwiched between the dense, unending pine trees on either side with no lights.

We got out of the car and walked in the darkness toward a clearing. The lunar light and our Bic lighters were our only illumination. It was quieter than any other place we had ever been, and the hum of our breathing was as loud and constant as the sound of feet crunching on twigs and brush. I was scared in a way I hadn't been since we had first started chasing ghosts. I couldn't tell if Liz was, but I didn't want to be that scared half who ran back to the car yet again.

As we walked to the clearing overlooking the water and the woods where the Leeds shack was supposed to sit, I wondered out loud what the shack would possibly look like. After three hundred years, it was hard to believe it would be intact enough to support all of the witnesses who had been to visit it. We moved on into the clearing and strained to find the facade in the dark. Squinting and flicking our lighters like manic fireflies, we scanned the area. I whispered that we must have gone too far or taken a wrong turn. We both stood in the dark for a while, not talking but listening to the sounds coming from the woods.

Liz whispered that the shack was gone. We should have known better. We should have come to see it years ago. They must have torn it down. I thought of all of the people who had claimed to have been to the shack as recently as last year, but the clearing was so overgrown it was evident that there hadn't been anything intact for years.

We left the clearing and headed back to the car. We didn't talk much as we pulled a K-turn out of the dead end, unable to see anything except for the small portion of road illuminated by the headlights. A profound disappointment burned, of driving this whole way with nothing to show for it. The stories still existed, but somewhere along the way the substance had disappeared.

Liz shouted for us to stop because she'd dropped her burning cigarette somewhere on the floor of the car. I stopped short and shut the car off as she scrambled to find it, using her lighter since my dome light switch was broken and neither of us dared open the door. The crisis was averted and we resumed being terrified, only slightly disarmed by the chaos. Then Liz screamed that she saw something run by the car.

We screamed some more when the car refused to start.

We finally calmed down and sat in the car, parked in the darkness and trying to make out any discernible shapes outside. I thought about all of the urban legends that started out like this, with hook-hand convicts and phantom hitchhikers. And then headlights were coming toward us and we froze: it was a police car.

The cop pulled up alongside us and asked if we knew that we were trespassing on private property. I explained our car trouble, and he asked me to start the car. Of course, the engine turned over just fine and he directed us to get out of the car for a routine sobriety test. With two of us standing on a lonely dead-end road on one foot, we tried to explain that we hadn't come to the Pine Barrens to get high. So why were we twenty miles out of the way from our affluent suburb, offseason for the beach and looking guilty?

We told him we were out here for a glimpse of the Jersey Devil and that we had seen something run past the car. We were both shivering at the thought of it still being out there.

He laughed heartily and shook his head. Then he told us to get back in the car and make our way home. Before we took off, though, he motioned for me to roll down my window.

"You know," he whispered, looking over his shoulder, "you really shouldn't be out here looking for that thing. It's real, you know. My cousin's husband grew up here, and *he's seen it.*"

As we pulled away, we turned up Springsteen on the radio, laughing and singing along about his hometown. The Pine Barrens fell away into the vacuum of unlit pavement behind us, the sense of comfort from escaping fear and possible death blanketing our charged bodies. The bond between us was palpable once again.

A week after our drive to the Barrens, a ringing phone in the early morning jolted me from dreams of college in New York City. On the other end, Liz's mother cried nearly inaudibly. That morning, she'd found her daughter facedown in her bed, not breathing, dead of a heroin overdose. It was the sound of the alarm clock that had driven her to investigate Liz's bedroom, a blaring that had gone on and on, without end. It seems Liz had set it the night before so she could get up early to shop for a prom dress. Unbelieving, I bolted over to her house, treading the same path I had for the past five years, desperate for proof. A lone police car idled in front of her house and the coroner pulled into her driveway as I moved through the front door and into the arms of her sobbing mother. Numbness set in; death was now something that happened to us.

Three weeks later, the night before graduation, I sat in the living room of my house, looking out onto her window. Sitting in the darkness, gripping the purple flashlight, I surveyed our front yards, the patch of pavement where we had pricked our fingers, and the street that had witnessed our escapes so many times.

I waited for her parents' bedroom to go dark. When it did, I turned on the flashlight—two fast flickers—and waited. Hours passed, but the window remained black. I tried it again the following night and then every night after that until I went away to school and could no longer send our signal.

A decade later, I still wonder if someday there will be a legend about a seventeen-year-old girl on the brink of her graduation who went to bed and never woke up again. It would be a story about a girl who lived fearlessly but burned out too quickly to realize life beyond our turnpike exit. I imagine the retelling whispered around campfires, the hushed stories: supposedly, if you sit in the dark house across the street facing hers and signal two times, she will answer with three short lights, letting you know she is stuck inside forever and cannot sneak out.

To this day, I've never seen Liz, the Jersey Devil, or any ghosts, for that matter, but I've watched so many times, hoping, waiting. Should she ever show up, I will not be afraid.

# NEW JERSEY: THE MOVIE

## ADAM LOWENSTEIN

EXIT 9

Nothing could be less cinematic than New Jersey. Movies, after all, are the stuff of dreams, of impossibly beautiful people and untouchably exotic places. Hollywood's old reputation as "the dream factory" stubbornly persists to this day, and nothing could be further from these dreams, geographically or spiritually, than New Jersey. For most Americans, New Jersey conjures images of toxic waste, faceless shopping malls, and torturous traffic—the kinds of things that encourage people to disparage New Jersey as "the armpit of the nation" and conclude that the license-plate moniker of "Garden State" must be the result of either cruel sarcasm or delusional thinking.

But for me, New Jersey is where my own passion for cinema was born. Today, as a professor of film studies, I can trace a direct line from my awakening to movies while growing up in New Jersey to the work I feel lucky to devote myself to each day. While watching the recent wave of movies set in the Garden State, I've become particularly fascinated by how "the armpit of the nation" has carved out a unique cinematic identity for itself. In the last ten years or so, New Jersey has laid claim to its own little corner of the dream factory's imagination, even if that corner usually exists in the neighborhood of semi-independent, modestly budgeted cinema rather than the realm of Hollywood blockbusters (as if to prove the point, notice how Bayonne is the first place to be annihilated in Steven Spielberg's *War of the Worlds*). What I want to reflect on is how New Jersey became cinematic *because* of its mythic awfulness, not despite it; to ask, in other words, whether I have become a film studies professor because of New Jersey or despite it.

I'd like to begin my admittedly idiosyncratic rather than comprehensive panorama of recent Jersey cinema with *Cop Land*. At several crucial junctures in this offbeat thriller, a New Jersey sheriff played by Sylvester Stallone looks out across the Hudson River toward the towering spectacle of Manhattan. Stallone, who in *Cop Land* has been transformed from a muscle-bound Rocky/Rambo into a dumpy, half-deaf, hopelessly single loser stuck in the sticks of North Jersey, spends most of the film observing New York as the place beyond his grasp. All the ruined promise and cowardly decisions in his life seem to be captured in that maddening gap, physically negligible but emotionally cavernous, between New York and New Jersey. If only he could stand up for himself, the film suggests, maybe he could graduate from New Jersey to New York, from passive to active, from loser to winner.

As if Stallone's predicament were not humiliating enough, he is also caught between two much more powerful, self-assured cops, the murderously corrupt Harvey Keitel and the crusading internal affairs watchdog Robert De Niro. The fact that Stallone, who has never really been given his due as a "serious actor," must face off against two of the most accomplished icons of the New York acting world only heightens our sense that he is doomed, that the odds stacked against him are insurmountable. How can "New Jersey" (not just the state but the state of mind) ever hope to compete with "New York"?

Of course, *Cop Land* is still a movie, even if it is set in New Jersey. So it should not surprise anyone when Stallone finally arrives, bloody but unbowed, on the steps of De Niro's Manhattan office to deliver the case-saving fugitive personally. In the film's final minutes, Stallone again gazes at New York from the Jersey side, but we understand that his vision is no longer tainted with crippling fear or impossible longing. He has found himself at last, so there is no longer any need to cross the river physically—he has traversed it spiritually and come home.

For all its heavy-handed clumsiness, *Cop Land* resonates with me. It reminds me how, in a fit of my own heavy-handedness, I pushed for "Across the River" as the theme that would organize our high school yearbook. It was 1989, my senior year at Highland Park High School in Highland Park,

New Jersey. I was convinced that it was my responsibility as one of the yearbook editors to persuade the rest of the editorial board that "Across the River" captured something essential about our experiences in Highland Park—a small, middle-class town in Central Jersey located across the Raritan River from the city of New Brunswick, the headquarters of both Rutgers University and the Johnson & Johnson corporation. But part of what attracted me to the "Across the River" theme was the sense that it crystallized something important not just about Highland Park but about New Jersey itself. After all, crossing the river south of Highland Park would bring you into New Brunswick, but taking the train or driving less than an hour north would take you across another river into New York City. As the kind of obsessive overachiever who hoped that various editorial stints on the yearbook and high school newspaper and a spot on a regional swim team and a tutoring job in the school's writing center and a GPA near the top of my class would somehow compensate for a family life marred by my parents' recent divorce and a hapless romantic life of my own, the grand theme of "Across the River" had an irresistible appeal for me. Like my hometown and my home state, I was striving frantically for some kind of legitimacy that seemed so achingly close but not quite close enough—always just the other side of somewhere else.

New Jersey as "elsewhere," as the place peripheral to the center, is a theme explored again and again in recent Jersey films. Stallone's gaze across the Hudson in *Cop Land* is mirrored by Ryan Phillippe's longing looks toward Manhattan from Jersey City in *54*, and Kevin Smith's *Jersey Girl* begins by suggesting that the entire world can be divided into two categories: "New York" and "New Jersey." In true fairy-tale fashion, *Jersey Girl* goes on to depict New York as the seductive but ultimately evil place of soul-sucking, self-centered ambition and New Jersey as the staid but finally good place of life-affirming family connections. Here New Jersey emerges as the authentic to New York's plastic, the real to New York's unreal.

The best moments in *Jersey Girl* recognize this kind of dualism as fantasy, as the stuff of fairy tales. Think of the hilarious job interview Ben Affleck must endure at the hands of two New York PR industry types brought to life through inspired cameos by Matt Damon and Jason Lee. Affleck, stripped of his former New York professional credentials and exiled to New Jersey, could hardly be more cluelessly earnest in his "Jerseyness" next to Damon and Lee's over-the-top, petty dismissiveness as "New Yorkers." The most strained moments in the film arise when Smith wants us to take these fairy-tale depictions of "New York" and "New Jersey" *seriously*—when we are asked to believe in megastars like Affleck and Liv Tyler embodying some kind of heartfelt Jersey authenticity that makes New York seem small. In these moments it seems that Smith, who has explored the subject of New Jersey before to more intriguing effect in *Clerks* and *Chasing Amy,* forgets how complicated the notion of Jersey "authenticity" really is.

When I had to speak to Highland Park about Highland Park during my high school graduation (as salutatorian of my class—just this side of valedictorian, of course), I mentioned that along with the very real joys made possible by the tightly knit community of a small town, such as pulling together during tragic losses, there were some daunting frustrations. These obstacles to happiness, which I dared to describe only with gentle euphemisms in my speech, included being doomed to pursue the same girl in high school that you had swooned for in fifth grade (yet never really date her) and having no movie theater available to walk to (although I could dimly recall a New Brunswick venue called the Art Cinema that seemed to advertise foreign and/or X-rated films, but it was razed before I was even old enough to try to sneak in). At the time, the idea of a town without a movie theater seemed too small, too real, too authentic, too New Jersey. I knew that Highland Park's small-town authenticity mattered when it counted most, but that this same authenticity could also feel suffocating.

Of course, one cannot speak of New Jersey authenticity and its attendant paradoxes without invoking Bruce Springsteen. Both *Cop Land* and *Jersey Girl* make conspicuous use of Springsteen songs on their sound tracks, with the latter even borrowing its title from a Tom Waits song made legendary by Springsteen. The inclusion of Springsteen's music in both of these films gives them direct access to the aura of Jersey authenticity that they depend upon. Springsteen, more than any other figure in contemporary popular culture, puts New Jersey on the map of America and projects that map to the world. On Springsteen's map, New Jersey stands for real, everyday, working-class people—a romantic vision of authenticity synonymous with America at its honest best and thus ripe for cinematic adaptation. Or is it? On a closer look, Springsteen's songs understand the double bind of authenticity and suffocation in ways that his mass popularity, especially at its height during the 1980s, seems to deny. The most famous example of this denial was President Ronald Reagan's attempt to hijack Springsteen's image as "American" for his own political ends—something that could be imagined only by someone so oblivious to the searing anger behind a song like "Born in the U.S.A." that he mistakes it for triumphalism. In fact, the cinematic inspiration one detects most often in Springsteen's own music belongs to films like *The Night of the Hunter*, *Badlands*, and *The Deer Hunter*—films with stunningly dark renderings of small-town, "authentic" America.

In this sense, Springsteen's haunting "Stolen Car," the song that appears in *Cop Land*, is ultimately more in keeping with the spirit (if not the subject matter) of one of the most striking cinematic testaments to New Jersey authenticity as suffocation: Todd Solondz's *Welcome to the Dollhouse*. When Springsteen sings of a man who must "travel in fear" so often that he worries he may just "disappear" into the darkness, his words bear a remarkable resemblance to the nightmarish adolescent experiences of Dawn Wiener (played by Heather Matarazzo) in *Dollhouse*. Dawn, a painfully awkward eleven-year-old, seems doomed to wander alone in a world set against her—her classmates terrorize her, her teachers despise her, and even her own parents favor her ambitious older brother and angelic younger sister. Even though Solondz refrains from citing New Jersey explicitly within this jet black comedy, the aura of the Garden State is palpable. New York looms over the film as a place of both escape and danger, the city where Dawn's dream boyfriend plans to establish his (illusory) musical career and to which her (momentarily) actual boyfriend runs away after being expelled for alleged drug dealing. Most important, New York becomes Dawn's destination after her sister is kidnapped—an event that the resentful Dawn has a hand in causing. Dawn travels to Times Square with the dream of finding her sister, fantasizing that she will rescue her from her depraved, homeless abductor and receive the undying gratitude of her family, school, and community.

The reality looks very different. Her sister is found (apparently unmolested) in the basement of a neighbor who had always appeared trustworthy, Dawn's flight to New York is never even noticed by her family, and when Dawn speaks at a school assembly to thank everyone for their support during her sister's disappearance, they heckle her with taunting chants of "Wienerdog." Once again, New Jersey plays the authentic to New York's inauthentic, but this time the unmasking of Jersey reality beside New York fantasy highlights just how cruel and crushing the authentic can be. Not surprisingly, the ad copy on the videocassette jacket of *Dollhouse* seems more reminiscent of Ronald Reagan on Bruce Springsteen than the content of the film itself: *"Welcome to the Dollhouse* is a stark, suburban comedy about 11 year old Dawn Wiener, a middle child in middle school in the middle of New Jersey . . . [who] does find moments of grace amidst the pain and humiliation of her first series of frustrated love affairs, and soon begins to wonder if life might not be better outside New Jersey."

Despite its misleading wishful thinking, the *Dollhouse* ad copy evokes a classic and powerful Jersey narrative: the redemptive escape from the state to "that place where we really want to go" (as Springsteen puts it in "Born to Run,"

New Jersey's not-quite-official state song). I was not immune to the temptations of this narrative myself when it came time to plan my own transition from high school to college. Although it made abundant practical and financial sense to attend Rutgers, the fine state university of New Jersey, where my father's faculty position would grant me free tuition, I could not bear the idea of college as a sequel to Highland Park High School, complete with similar faces (many of my classmates would matriculate at Rutgers) and familiar settings (it was one thing to wax poetic about the metaphors of "across the river" in high school; it was quite another to contemplate walking across the not very wide Raritan River as my rite of passage from high school to college). So I schemed and fought to avoid Rutgers at any cost and eventually succeeded in enrolling at the University of Virginia, a college that seemed to my mind brimming with all the mystical promise of escape that Springsteen sang about in "Born to Run" when he dreamed of a "walk in the sun."

But it was not until I stood, alone and apart from the ecstatic crowd at a UVA fraternity party where the band had just launched into Lynyrd Skynyrd's "Sweet Home Alabama," that I felt like I truly identified with "Born to Run." Suddenly, it seemed as though what Springsteen meant about "that place where we really want to go" was not an actual paradise outside of New Jersey but some kind of inner place where you can confidently stake a claim to who you are. And who I was, I realized then with a proud certainty that eludes Dawn in *Welcome to the Dollhouse*, was a kid from New Jersey.

If my "escape" to Virginia only brought me closer to the Garden State, it was through a road trip not just across the miles but into the heart of identity itself. This theme also surfaces, against all expectation, in the comedy *Harold & Kumar Go to White Castle.* Harold Lee (played by John Cho), an overly responsible Korean-American investment banking analyst, and his roommate, Kumar Patel (played by Kal Penn), a barely responsible Indian-American medical-student-to-be, leave their Hoboken apartment in a marijuana-fueled quest for the perfect munchies meal: the hamburgers served up by the White Castle fast-food chain. Their madcap search for the elusive White Castle takes them all over New Jersey, with stops including Newark, New Brunswick, Princeton, Freehold, and Cherry Hill and encounters with everyone from horny evangelical Christians to diarrhea-afflicted Princeton coeds to *Doogie Howser, M.D.*'s Neil Patrick Harris on Ecstasy. *Harold & Kumar* relishes its place in the raunchy teen comedy tradition immortalized by movies such as *Animal House* and *American Pie,* but it also spins that tradition to fascinating effect by placing on center stage the nonwhite characters usually relegated to the margins of those films (if present at all).

The fact that this movement from margin to center in *Harold & Kumar* occurs against the backdrop of that most "marginal" of states ("the armpit of the nation") lends a certain gravity to the parade of sex, drugs, and bodily functions gags. The Jersey setting, so strongly associated with the "authentic," almost demands that the film return to the darker, more troubling aspects of its premise each time it threatens to disappear into the mists of fantasy. Sprinkled throughout the film are scenes that remind the audience how risky and humiliating it can be to live as a nonwhite person in a "white-as-normal" America and that Harold and Kumar's quest for *White* Castle has more bittersweet and ambivalent overtones than may at first appear.

In certain ways, the background of New Jersey helps keep Harold and Kumar honest, vulnerable, and flawed; in this sense, they share something with the often thwarted mobsters of the New Jersey–set cable television phenomenon *The Sopranos*. Tony Soprano and his comrades are a distinctively "Jersey" version of the Mafia, acutely aware of their increasingly anachronistic status in the world and the vast distance that separates them from "glorious" mobsters like those portrayed in the *Godfather* films. The opening credits of *The Sopranos* depict Tony driving along the roads of New Jersey, the Manhattan skyline passing by his window, as he makes his way home to an affluent suburb. It is significant that the first glimpses we get of Tony, like the dominant images we remember of Harold and Kumar, show us the context of driving through New Jersey—a place, perhaps (and for these characters especially), with more roads to drive than destinations that can be reached.

I realize that my accounts of *Welcome to the Dollhouse* and *Harold & Kumar Go to White Castle* may finally concentrate too narrowly on their more serious aspects at the expense of their many comedic flourishes. This is only because both of these films, in their own ways, so forcefully tap into my own recognition while growing up that the idea of New Jersey as safe "home" distinct from New York's dangerous "away" can exist only as a mirage. There were a number of fatal accidents and premature deaths in our small Highland Park community that unsettled any sense of safety, but none as shocking as the murder of our high school principal, William Donahue, at the hands of a former student who had been romantically involved with his daughter. Donahue had stepped in during an argument at his home between his daughter and her troubled ex-boyfriend, who then stabbed him to death. The violent loss of our principal, a charismatic man who inhabited his administrative role with a graceful combination of humor and resolve, convulsed our entire town. I remember the overwhelming sight of star athletes on our high school teams, the kind of guys who always strutted so confidently through the hallways between classes, crying openly while they spoke with the volunteer team of psychologists and social workers that descended on our school in the wake of the murder. Teachers and staff tried to reassure us that some kind of order would return to the everyday life of the school, but many of them could not get through such reassurances without fighting back tears of their own.

In our current post-Columbine and talk show–saturated culture, I'm not sure that Donahue's death would even register very far outside the confines of Highland Park. But back in 1987, it had a brief moment as national news. There was even a feature story in the *New York Times Magazine* (written by a graduate of Highland Park High School) about the impact of Donahue's murder on our town. Donahue's absence in our high school was painfully real—the disappearance of his voice on the intercom every morning to deliver the school announcements in his signature style (signing off with a phrase like "Learn something today" with just the right note of genuine conviction, the kind that even teenage cynicism couldn't quite dispel) was a daily reminder of the fact of his death. But

reading the *Times* story felt surreal, as if somet[...]
tablished order of things had gone horribly, b[...]
Highland Park was expected to exist in the [...]
York, too tiny and nondescript and insignifica[...]
metropolis ever to notice. Living in the shadow of N[...]
may have often felt frustrating, but it was understood on some
level to be a small price to pay for the security and intimacy
provided by our small town that the buzzing, impersonal
chaos of New York could not hope to offer. Donahue's murder
shattered that promise. We were supposed to read about the
violence of New York; New York was not supposed to read
about the violence of Highland Park.

Of course, the opportunity to entertain such illusions of
safety in the first place was a privilege of living in a middle-
class Jersey town. It was the kind of privilege unthinkable in
many sections of New Brunswick, and in the Newark captured in the gritty film *New Jersey Drive*. But at the time, my
sense of "home" as familiar and stable, already shaken by my
parents' divorce, was cracked wide open. How would I recover? How would Highland Park recover?

There's something at the core of Zach Braff's *Garden State*
that speaks more eloquently about the answers to these questions than I could myself by narrating the happenings of my
life or my hometown's history. Braff, directing himself as the
twenty-something Andrew Largeman, comes home to New
Jersey from Los Angeles to bury his mother. Largeman,
known by the nickname "Large" to the eccentric crew of
friends he left behind in Jersey when he embarked on a career
as an actor, is not a very "large man" at all. His acting career is
at a standstill, his grip on his day job as a waiter is tenuous,

.d, worst of all, he has been on such a long and steady diet of antidepressants that he has trouble feeling anything whatsoever. His father, who is also his psychiatrist and the dispenser of his medication, cannot find a way to communicate with his son. In fact, they have never truly spoken to each other about the event that has defined their lives most powerfully: the accident during Andrew's boyhood that left his mother paralyzed. Andrew's father, and sometimes Andrew himself, believes it was Andrew who caused this accident.

Andrew's sense of detachment from his own life motivates both the richly humorous and the genuinely wrenching moments of *Garden State*. We are disturbed by his inability to cry at his mother's funeral, but we cannot help but laugh afterward when a friend of his mother's presents him with an unintentionally perfect gift—a shirt that matches the wallpaper of his parents' home exactly. Like Dawn in *Welcome to the Dollhouse,* Andrew has no true home, no place of familiar safety where he can recover from the world that overwhelms him. But unlike Dawn, Andrew finds someone who gives him that shot at recovery, a way out of being alone. When he meets Sam (played by Natalie Portman) during his visit back home, he feels drawn to this striking but odd young woman with a compulsion for lying. The heart of the film concerns the quirky friendship and eventual romance between Andrew and Sam—a playful, sometimes crazy, but finally deep and courageous coming together of two people who find in each other the means to face the pain of their own lives.

In one of the film's most ambitious sequences, Andrew, Sam, and Andrew's friend Mark (played by Peter Sarsgaard) embark on a kind of Jersey odyssey connected to Andrew's loss of his mother. Mark leads them from a soulless shopping center to a seedy motel to a failed construction site tended by a family who live in awe of the cavernous underground abyss at the site's center. The sequence culminates with the three wanderers, exhausted and rain-soaked, screaming into the abyss and laughing together—in frustration, in delirium, but finally in a kind of shared joy. Nietzsche warned that "when you look into the abyss, the abyss also looks into you," and the odyssey undertaken by Andrew, Sam, and Mark has forced them to stare into a personal darkness that has been mapped onto the drab, disheartening sights of New Jersey. But here at the climax of the sequence, when the abyss becomes literal, it reveals itself as something else. Yes, it's a construction site that threatens to swallow the godforsaken sprawl that surrounds it, but it's also a thing of wonder and even unexpected beauty—like the Garden State itself. The abyss has indeed looked into them, but they share the danger of the darkness rather than become consumed by it. During this scene, the film's title seems to refer not only to the state of New Jersey but also to the promise of beginnings, however unlikely.

I happened to see *Garden State* during its opening weekend in limited release, at a small neighborhood theater in Maplewood, New Jersey, that was the only venue outside New York City screening the film at that time (Maplewood is near the town of South Orange, where Braff grew up). I didn't really plan to see it the night I did. My girlfriend and I, living in Brooklyn at the time, were back in New Jersey for the day visiting relatives. After seeing one side of my family at a gathering in Passaic, we decided quite spontaneously that we wanted to see the film that night—and not in New York, but in New Jersey. The show we tried to make was sold out, so we bought tickets for the late show and spent the next couple of hours strolling the streets of Maplewood together.

Highland Park is not very far from Maplewood, but I had never been there before. As we walked the few blocks of businesses in the center of this small town—an ice cream shop, a French restaurant, a modest bookstore already closed for the evening—I thought about all the resemblances to my hometown. I asked my girlfriend if she noticed how similar so many of the houses here looked next to the homes I had introduced her to in Highland Park. She nodded and agreed, but for some reason I decided not to speak about the one difference between the two towns that was most significant to me at that instant. It was a major point of distinction, yet it was also the thing that made me feel most at home here: the presence of the movie theater itself. I reached out for her hand as we headed back toward the cinema, somehow certain that the choice we had made to see *Garden State* in the Garden State was an important one. After all, what could be more cinematic than this very moment?

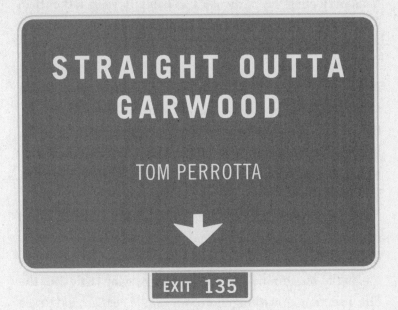

# STRAIGHT OUTTA GARWOOD

## TOM PERROTTA

EXIT 135

It was the summer of 1975. I was 13—too young to have a job but old enough to get into trouble—looking anxiously toward my first year of high school. My friends and I were killing another muggy day at the Garwood Little League, dividing our time between halfhearted games of Ping-Pong and Nok-Hockey (courtesy of the Town Rec. Department) and wholehearted ogling of girls in their tube tops and cutoffs.

Something mysterious had happened to the girls we hung out with that summer. They had become suddenly unfamiliar, almost exotic—barefoot hippies with garish eye shadow who smoked their Marlboro Lights like old pros, like they'd been perfecting this particular bad habit for years rather than weeks—and my buddies and I spent a lot of time pondering their transformation.

At some point—maybe it was the lull after lunch—I found myself alone with M., this very cool guy who was about to begin his junior year at David Brearley Regional. To me, though, M. might as well have been a grown man, with his long hair and Stephen Stills muttonchops, not to mention his reputation for selling pot and getting his girlfriends to go further with him than they'd gone with anyone else.

A year or so later, he would discover the Grateful Dead the way some people find religion and would drift out of Garwood and out of my life. But just then he was sitting next to me on the playground swings, our feet swaying lazily over the dirt. I remember wishing there were some girls around to see us together, to register the fact that he seemed to regard me as someone worth talking to.

"Didja ever hear of this guy Bruce Springsteen?" he asked. I shook my head. The name meant nothing to me.

"He's pretty cool," M. informed me. "Kinda like Dylan, except he writes about people like us."

It's funny how a casual remark like that—he writes about people like us—can stick with you for thirty years. It didn't make that much of an impression on me at the time, beyond making me commit Bruce's name to memory, which of course turned out to be completely unnecessary, since "Born to Run" was released a month later and nobody my age from New Jersey ever had to be asked if they'd heard of that guy Springsteen again.

It wasn't until I got to college and began to seriously consider writing as a possible career that I began reflecting on the actual substance of M.'s remark. What did it mean, for Springsteen, or anyone else, to write about people like us? Were people like us—whoever we were—actually worth writing about?

What made it even more complicated was that Springsteen's characters seemed so oddly familiar and otherworldly at the same time. They drove souped-up cars down the parkway and wandered the same boardwalks as the rest of us, but they seemed bigger than we were, full of romantic yearnings and desperate poetry that I'd never heard anyone express in the long, straight halls of my high school or inside the brightly lit stores of the Woodbridge Mall.

In my first creative writing classes at Yale, I wrote some stories based loosely on people I knew or had heard about in Garwood—a lonely barber, musicians in a high school rock band called the Antennas, a girl who secretly despises her popular jock boyfriend—and they were received with gratifying enthusiasm by my classmates, for many of whom the blue-collar "swamps of Jersey" were as foreign as the steppes of Russia. The stories came easily to me—almost too easily. It felt a little like cheating, like I wasn't using my imagination.

So for the next few years I tried to be what I considered a real fiction writer, to make things up, to set stories in places where I hadn't lived and populate them with characters I hadn't grown up knowing. I wrote about political dissidents in unnamed Eastern European countries and suburban wives who have affairs with the handsome Scandinavian tennis pro at "the club." I tried to integrate elements of Latin American magic realism into my stories, with predictably embarrassing results.

By the time I got to graduate school—I had been admitted into the Creative Writing Program at Syracuse—I was floundering. Like many of my classmates, I had a vocation, but not a subject. That is, I could write in theory, but I had nothing in particular to write about, no story that only I could tell. Right in the thick of my literary identity crisis, I watched a few episodes of a new show called *The Wonder Years,* which was set during the era of my childhood. It was sweet and funny and nostalgic, and something about it made me angry. That wasn't what it was like, I thought. They're leaving all the important stuff out.

So I started writing some stories set in a fictional town called Darwin, New Jersey, which had more than a few things in common with the real town of Garwood, New Jersey. All the stories were narrated by a young kid named Buddy, and they dealt with the kinds of events you wouldn't normally see on network TV: a girl who refuses to say the Pledge of Allegiance, a boy who steals from his stepfather's gas station, an unprovoked act of racial violence. Buddy loses his virginity to a girl in his driver's ed class and unwittingly takes a lesbian to the senior prom.

As hard-edged as the stories can be, they're infused with a comic energy that seems to me to be one of the essential qualities of the collective New Jersey mind-set. In the Garden State, we don't just laugh at the funny stuff—we laugh about the sad stuff and the awful stuff, too. It doesn't make it any less sad or awful, just a little easier to face.

These stories, ten in all, were collected in my first book,

*Bad Haircut.* And just like that, I had found my subject, my identity. I was a New Jersey writer, a guy from Garwood, writing about things that happened there, or could have. In my next book, *The Wishbones,* I wrote about a group of wedding musicians—a little bit like some talented guys I grew up with—who were facing the onset of responsible adulthood and the possible end of their rock 'n' roll dreams. In *Election,* I set a story of high school politics and corruption against the backdrop of the Glen Ridge rape case. After that came *Joe College,* a semiautobiographical novel about a kid from small-town, blue-collar New Jersey—the son of a guy who drives a lunch truck called "The Roach Coach"—who goes to Yale and has to learn to navigate between two very different cultures.

The irony is that during all of this, during a whole decade of thinking of myself first and foremost as a New Jersey writer, I wasn't living in New Jersey but in Brooklyn and then Connecticut and then outside Boston. In my most recent book, *Little Children,* I finally faced up to the fact of my exile and told a story set in the suburbs of Massachusetts.

A few months after *Little Children* was published, though, I returned to Garwood for my twenty-fifth high school reunion. A number of my classmates had read some of my books or had at least seen the movie version of *Election.* But if they had a question for me, it was almost always about *Bad Haircut.* Was that character based on Bobby or Mark? What about that guy in the white Camaro? Is that who I think it is?

As a rule, fiction writers don't like it when readers look for a one-to-one correspondence between literature and real life. They think it's insulting, as if the person asking the question doesn't want to give the writer credit for having an imagination. But I wasn't insulted, even when my classmates were wildly off-base about the inspiration for a particular character. I couldn't help feeling like they were paying me the same compliment M. had paid to Bruce Springsteen on that summer day in 1975: they were saying that, for better or worse, I had at least written about the world we'd lived in, that the characters in my stories were people we might have known, people like us.

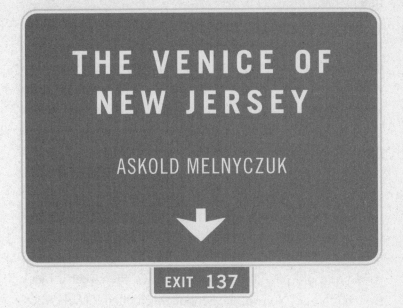

# THE VENICE OF NEW JERSEY

## ASKOLD MELNYCZUK

EXIT 137

**S**ex was discovered in New Jersey in the summer of 1962. I don't know what people did before then—you'll have to check with someone else. In any case, I made it a point to instruct as many of my approximate peers as I could in this ancient knowledge before finally retiring to the country of marriage. While my students were mostly girls my age, my teacher had been a male family friend nearly a decade older. I recall telling my mother about it on the eve of my First Communion while trying to figure out what to say to the priest during confession. She assured me this fit the bill. Fortunately, Father Bodnar figured three Hail Marys pretty much covered things. The subject never came up again, which was fine by me.

My first teacher's texts included gaudy colored pics clipped from so-called girlie magazines of the period—the relatively innocent, pre-Kennedy assassination sixties, not long after we'd moved from the triple-decker in Irvington to the huge single-family in Cranford, a small town built along the Rahway River and known as the Venice of New Jersey. Who first called it that I don't know, but the inspiration behind the baptism couldn't have been clearer: nearly every year April's showers swelled the Rahway until it spilled over its banks, flooding the streets for several blocks. For many resourceful New Jerseyans this was an invitation to test out their floats, inflatable mattresses, and canoes. I seem to remember the sight of neighbors young and old paddling cheerfully down the street a block from our house. None of the gondoliers crooned "O Sole Mio," though. By the time I docked at high school, the river had been successfully dammed and banked (because of course what delighted the boaters was no picnic for those with homes along the river's edge) and the waters receded. Our suburban town became more a mini Milan, with its banks and sweet shops, than a toy Venice. My desire for sexual experience, however, gone more or less underground for nearly a decade after that early initiation, was not so easily contained.


It must be the chemicals in the air, or perhaps it's sheer population density, that explains why New Jersey has been the site of so many fortuitous finds and inventions. Edison's Menlo Park was less than a dozen miles from us. As late as the early seventies, one of his plants still stood in Roselle, right next door. In Morristown to this day stands the Speedwell Ironworks, where in 1838 Samuel Morse and his partner, Alfred Vail, developed the telegraph. "A patient waiter is no loser," their first message read. Seven miles from Cranford, Newark, called the most beautiful city in America in 1850, was home to that iconic American innovation: plastic. Heading south, central New Jersey spawned the Institute for Advanced Studies at Princeton, where Einstein rooted in his old age. The father of one of my closest high school friends was one of the chemists who perfected the kind of nylon used in stockings. But it was Jersey, where genius sprang from the earth in all weathers and seasons.

Nothing less than love itself was also first discovered in New Jersey—in Cranford, in the spring of 1972, to be exact. Between my induction into the cult by my family's friend and my second significant step along the way, the mustard seed of desire had been watered by the Miracle-Gro of a hypersexualized culture, flowering at last in my senior year, when Alma, surely the most beautiful girl at Cranford High, far out of my league socially and in every other way, heard I'd gotten into college and so took pity on me. Because she had a regular boyfriend several years older, from the far tougher neighboring city of Newark, her gift would be passed on in secret, reinforcing my sense that somehow eros was best honored, like God, in silence. (Later, in college, in a profaner mood, I memorized and recited lines from a poem by Mark Strand: "There is a girl you like so you tell her your penis is big.")

So one rainy Sunday afternoon in April, knowing my parents had gone directly from church to New York to see a play at Joe Papp's Public Theater, Alma arrived. I sensed my parents taking their seats the very moment Alma slipped off her light, red silk jacket. I opened the window to release our cigarette smoke. After a respectable ten minutes of chat, we got down to what had brought us together. First, I unfolded the black vinyl convertible sofa on which I'd slept for five years. (The room's two previous occupants, my grandfather and the paternal grandmother Father had imported from Ukraine in 1963, had both died there, and it had been decided it would be bad luck for me to sleep in their bed.) I put my one Byrds album on the Blaupunkt in the living room and cranked the volume up, loud enough so that our own voices wouldn't disturb my sister in the room next door or my cousins, aunt, and uncle downstairs. Living in a house surrounded by so many people, several of whom are always in residence, teaches you to create solitude amid crowds. In our home, someone was always sneaking smokes, sex, and swigs—as if it really were possible to hide anything, though for the sake of harmony, for good and ill, people mostly played along, despite the frequent psychological short-circuiting of the inhabitants. But they, along with the rest of New Jersey, melted away the minute I first saw Alma's breasts, and then she was under the sheets while I, still dressed, attended to the security arrangements surrounding our moment.

I was down to my underwear and had lit a joint as "Eight Miles High" enveloped us in chords primed for ecstasy. At last the stars had aligned.

A knock on the door snapped me out of my fugue state.

I threw a body block to keep my sister from entering.

"What?"

"That was Mom on the phone."

I had heard no ring.

"They've walked out of the play. Said it was filthy. They'll be home in half an hour."

I looked at Alma in panic, despair, and relief. Her dark, Sephardic eyes blinked at me uncomprehendingly.

"We can be quick," Alma offered.

No, I insisted, I wanted us to be able to take our time, to luxuriate in the fullness of our sensual beings. I wanted to love her the way she deserved—a thing I had no idea how to do.

Alma stared back, confused, maybe hurt—but I hadn't yet unlearned the *homerta* our strict Greek Catholic immigrant household placed on the subject of sex. Do what you must, but don't talk about it, ever. I watched her sheathe her breasts in her bra and pull down her sweater. While she slipped reluctantly back into the red silk jacket, I pretended to curse, though I suspect I felt more relief than rage. I walked her down the dark stairs leading out of the house. The rain had stopped, the air was cool, and as we leaned forward to kiss, our thwarted passion made her look more beautiful and desirable than ever. A little later, sitting by the window, I heard my parents' car pull in, while my eyes followed the trail of light Alma had left along Claremont Place and up North Union. At night, it glowed like a phosphorescent strip.

So it was that art thwarted life, briefly postponing the final consummation of the good work we had begun that Sunday. But I knew that the river of longing on which we'd paddled so far but no farther had merely dipped underground again. It would emerge before long as a torrent, and no levee of rules, commandments, or warnings would hold it.

And I was right.

Every patient waiter loses if he waits too long.


These days, reading about the abstinence movements in vogue among teens—or, more likely, among the fantasies of adults herding the kids together—I compare them to the spirit ruling my own raucous youth, which continued in the same vein for quite a while—blissful lawlessness, licit and abundant sex—and I wonder what they have gained and what I lost, and vice versa.

Was innocence stolen from me four decades ago by my teenage acquaintance? Not from my point of view. His life has been hard enough. Some years ago, after his mother, with whom he was living well into his forties, died, he had a breakdown. He was found by neighbors lying naked on the floor of the family living room, where he'd either collapsed or curled up hoping to will himself back to the only source of nourishment he'd ever known. After making a partial recovery, he had to leave New Jersey to live nearer relatives somewhere out west. *Pax vobiscum.* In general, I share the attitude Neruda articulated when he said he was born to love, not to judge, and I hope this man hasn't suffered any guilt on my account—and that Alma recalls our several trysts throughout that floodless spring and dry summer with a fraction of the fondness I feel for those two awkward kids.

Would my heart have broken less often had I stayed celibate until marriage? Might I have caused less emotional distress for the mindful men and women kind enough to have given me the time of day, and sometimes of night? Maybe. But it was the experience of having my heart broken over and again that taught me most of what I know about immortality and resurrection. "And as for love, love never ends," Paul wrote in that passage from Corinthians so many turn to when they speak their wedding vows. Had my heart never been broken, had I stayed celibate, had I not transgressed, perhaps I would have lived more conventionally, but could I ever have understood poetry or religion, those two great consolers of the brokenhearted? And without them, what would life be?

But New Jersey was the source of more than just sexual revelations. It was where the word "family" was defined in all its mythological complexity, reminding me that its root lies in the Latin for "servant" or "slave."

We must have loved that triple-decker in Roselle Park where I'd spent the first five years of my life, because when we moved to the Venice of New Jersey we promptly turned our gracious new home, with its large, first-floor living room and parlor, into one. The house was divvied up among three families. My Scottish aunt and her husband (my mother's brother), along with their three daughters, inhabited the first floor. My sister, my parents, and I occupied the second. The third was taken up by my then-unmarried Uncle Orest (my mother's youngest brother) and my maternal grandfather. A few years later, when my father succeeded in importing a grandmother from Ukraine, she joined them in that tiny attic room, rendered not merely habitable but even elegant by the imposition of faux wood paneling on the walls and ceiling.

My first memory of that house—in which my parents, an aunt, and a cousin still live—is tumbling down a flight of stairs the day we arrived, bumping past the wallpaper showing English hunting scenes, all the way to the bottom, then rising unscathed. I immediately fell in love with the large yard and the huge garage with the apartment above three bays that had once housed carriages and horses. A hitching post stood not far from the furnace in the barnlike back part my Uncle Orest promptly turned into a kind of petting zoo crowded with crated rabbits and ducks, where occasionally we'd find a horseshoe under the floorboards.

Orest, a natural gardener, made good use of that fertile Jersey soil—its fecundity the very incarnation of eros—by planting rows of apple, peach, and cherry trees around the blue, pink, and white hydrangeas. He also rooted a grapevine, which he quickly put to practical use by making his own Madeira. Another part of the yard became a productive garden for my Uncle Vlodyk, who seeded corn, tomatoes, squash, and various herbs, his prodigious efforts fueled by a tippling at the home brew. Exuberant and sociable, Vlodyk liked to sing along with his Mario Lanza records. Yet there was something of the hunted wolf about him—he'd been arrested by the Soviets while trying to avoid conscription into their army and had spent more than a year in Siberia. Fortunately, New Jersey's ecosystem accommodated a far greater variety of species—including lone wolves—than one might have guessed.

Many summer evenings, we—my three cousins, my sister, I, various friends, neighbors, adults (the house was a hive, never still)—played spud or freeze tag in the yard, watched over by a clan of raccoons as they licked themselves clean. Once a neighbor laid a trap out in his backyard, snaring the mother. My cousin Dierdre spotted the creature hobbling, the trap and chain dragging from its leg, into the garage. The group of us staked it out and waited for someone from the ASPCA, but by the time help arrived, all that remained of that bold, masked matriarch was the chain, the trap, and her hind leg, which she'd chewed off to get free. Three legs would do. For years afterward, we saw her with new litters of pups, taking the air on the roof those long summer evenings as we pursued fireflies, jars in hand, hoping the twilight might last forever and night never come, because all of us in that house were afflicted by nightmares, while in the long, unfurling hours before sleep, we counted ourselves kings of infinite space. There were dangers outside the borders of Claremont Place, but on its moonlit ground, we were safe.

The price of our safety had been steep. Chewing off a foot to get free of a trap isn't a bad metaphor for what exiles and immigrants sometimes do to survive. Today's debate on immigration, by focusing on what happens on this side of the border, fails to imagine what circumstances would drive someone to take such risks.

During a recent visit, as I walked down North Union Avenue to Riverside Drive, once the floodplains, with my eighty-six-year-old mother, I recalled earlier expeditions with her father, my grandfather. Together we stalked these same streets hunting for chestnuts dropped from the trees canopying the boulevard. What did I know of the world from which that octogenarian had fled? He had been captured near

Odessa and taken prisoner by the Bolsheviks in 1920. He survived an execution only because the sharpshooter was so drunk that he missed his target so many times he finally gave up. Afterward, Grandfather was conveyed to Moscow, where he somehow convinced Trotsky to allow him to save the icons of eastern Ukraine. But we didn't talk about any of that. He was a good man on a walk, and that was enough for me. We plunked our chestnuts in the pail and doled them out among the deserving back home.

Death—bitter, lonely, much-maligned death—first crept into my world in New Jersey. My initial encounter came when my imported grandmother died sitting up in a chair while waiting for my father to bring her her Sunday dinner. Hers had been a hard life. She was in her sixties when she came to the United States. She spoke no English and never found a place among the in-laws she met only on arriving here—she and my father had been separated by war when he was sixteen. We children mocked her—oh, the ruthless idyll of youth!—because she was fat, and old, and foreign. That January night, my cousins and I giggled as we stood in their wood-paneled dining room watching the funeral home guys lug her coffin down the stairs and out of the house; yet we recognized that something out of the ordinary had occurred. Two years later, when my grandfather passed, we knew enough to mourn. His was an exemplary exit—weakened and in pain, he never complained but wanted the newspaper read to him daily, saying in effect, as Paul wrote, "because love endureth all things, tell me, I pray thee, how fares the human race, if new roofs be risen on the ancient cities, whose empire is it now that sways the world . . ."

Twenty years later, after one of my best friends committed suicide, I began to look at death differently. No longer a member of my grandparents' generation, separated from me by an abyss of eons, death turned peer overnight. Now that we are members of the same tribe, I feel a grudging respect for it and hope for no less in return. After all, many died, but a few survived, and someone must tell the tale.

Having left the safety of Claremont Place thirty years ago, I can't begin to enumerate the experiences, good and bad, swept away by time's floods. This August, around the one-year anniversary of Hurricane Katrina, while visiting my parents, I was surprised by a headline in *The Eagle,* Cranford's newly renamed local paper: "Future of Flood Project in Doubt." It seemed that whatever solution the engineers had found decades ago was temporary, that in 1999 Hurricane Floyd had caused extensive damage. Now, however, various municipal, state, and federal agencies were dickering about whether to shore up the dams once again. Twenty million dollars was needed. Would the funds be found in time? Or would Cranford—like the rest of New Jersey, so transformed over the decades—win back its old reputation and name? Why not? The erotic aura around a Venetian theme park in New Jersey might be exploited for tourism. The town could buy glass-bottomed boats, import gondoliers who really could sing . . . for a minute the idea seemed almost charming. Then I remembered.

Because our house was on the crest of a very slight incline, so subtle it hardly deserves to be called a hill yet as a result of which the floodwaters never reached us, we were free to enjoy the strange sight of our neighbors, friends, and fellow Cranfordians sailing along the streets of the town, down North Union and up Riverside Drive. They traveled by tire, surfboard, and inflatable boat. However, my old friend Tom Bahr, with whom I fled the Garden State the day after graduating college in 1976, grew up on Cranford's Riverside Drive, and his memory of the floods was less romantic and playful. He recalls his father huffing and cursing as he dragged another box of waterlogged memories up to the living room while kids raced rubber rafts over the receding waters that ran down the streets along which, on most days, they pedaled bicycles, reminding me that in life, as in art, point of view is everything.

Which is why, as far as I'm concerned, birth, copulation, and death were all first discovered in New Jersey. To it go the blame, the praise, and the thanks.

**NEW JERSEY, 1963**

DANI SHAPIRO

EXIT 143B

They come in the night, setting fire to our front lawn, cars careening across our soft summer grass, tires digging dark grooves that will grow muddy and dank in the August heat. Their methods change with the seasons: In autumn, they toss raw eggs at the white columns of our house. In winter, they leave TV dinners filled with dog shit steaming in the snow outside our front door. In summer, the cars come screeching down the street, gaining momentum until they fly across our front lawn, ruining the sprinkler system my parents so proudly installed when they bought their piece of the American suburban dream.

I am asleep in my bed, in my pink-and-orange ruffled room with its shelves of dolls from foreign countries: Spanish dolls wearing layers of brightly colored skirts, wooden Russian dolls, tiny bowling pins of color which open up, revealing smaller and smaller versions of themselves inside. Downstairs, my parents are talking in hushed tones. Perhaps they are sitting in the living room, peering from behind the heavy brocade curtains at the arc of headlights flying across their lawn, as improbable as a shooting star. Maybe my mother calls the police, maybe not. They are used to this by now; they know the police do nothing.

Next to my parents, there is a glass case filled with ancient Judaica: blown glass from Jerusalem, antique silver wine goblets, parchment so old it crumbles to the touch. An intercom lets them hear me rustling in my bed. They look at each other, worry etched on their faces. They blame themselves, they blame one another, they blame history and the accident of geography that brought them to this neighborhood. Outside, there is a lone shout in the night—"Dirty Jews!"—and my father holds his head in his hands, fragile as an artifact.

Later that night, my mother checks on me. Her heels make soft thuds on the shag carpet of my room. Her breath is sweet and warm as she bends down and places a finger under my nose to make sure I'm still breathing. There is a mobile fluttering above my head and lithographs by Miró and Ben Shahn on the walls. The Ben Shahn has words on it, too, words I don't yet understand: *Who is God?*

• • •

I grew up in a house protected by three different kinds of alarm systems: A steady red light outside the front and back doors switched on by a small circular key. A motion detector in specific, supposedly crime-prone rooms, activated by currents in the air. And carefully placed "panic buttons"—one in my parents' bedroom and another in the kitchen. When pushed in unison, they set off an ear-splitting siren in the house and an alert to the local police of a crime in progress. As a child, I often wondered what would happen if, just for the hell of it, I pushed those buttons. Maybe, I thought, those buttons would make a bad situation worse.

We had alarm magnets on every window and alarm pads scattered throughout the house beneath the wall-to-wall carpeting like land mines. The inner doors all had push-button locks, and some of the telephones had a unique feature—a little plastic hinge which, if someone elsewhere in the house picked up an extension, would prevent them from listening in.

The key word was "protection." I don't know if this quest to seal us off from the rest of the world began before or after the violence and the screamed epithets in the night. But I have my hunches; my parents were both fearful people who believed that it was possible to control life, to keep the bogeyman away, to buy safety.

It was, I suppose, a piece of bad luck that my parents bought a house in a neighborhood where Jews weren't welcome. They were hardly kids when they married—well into their thirties and each divorced. Their decision to choose this particular house, this particular neighborhood, was a well-considered one. No doubt, they wasted hours debating the merits of the city versus the suburbs, New Jersey versus Connecticut. They wanted a home they could settle into, within commuting distance of the city and walking distance of a synagogue. My father, a born and bred Manhattanite, loved the idea of life in the suburbs.

I imagine them now, laying eyes on the Georgian colonial for the first time: the redbrick walls and white pillars, the flagstone walk winding up from the cobblestone street. A wrought-iron light hangs above the front door. They have driven from the city in my father's baby blue Chrysler, more boat than car, and they have brought my father's parents with them to see the house. I am an infant, bundled in my grandfather's arms. It is early spring; there are still icy patches on the ground, and my father steadies his father, holds on to his mother's elbow as they make their way around the back of the house, past two red brick lightposts that remind my mother of something she once saw in London. There are new trees in the backyard—a shady elm, a young oak—and my parents squeeze their clasped hands, imagining their family growing in this house, imagining these trees a few decades from now. In their mind's eye, the rooms are already being filled—they can see the teal velvet couch, the Eames chairs, the Ben Shahn lithograph in my room. My grandfather gives a nod of approval. "Now, this is *balebatish*," he says, this man whose own father was an immigrant and who now lives in a grand apartment on Central Park West. This is proper and beautiful.

When I close my eyes and try to breathe Hillside, New Jersey, back into my senses, I return to a place of immense contradiction: I smell the forsythia and the putrid smoke of nearby oil refineries, I hear the chirping of bluebirds in the backyard along with the roar of jets taking off from nearby Newark airport. Hillside was less a town than an enclave. There was no village, no Main Street, no general store. When people referred to "the city," they were talking about New York City. Though Manhattan was only half an hour away, to many of our neighbors it might as well have been halfway across the country. They saw it as a dangerous place—a place where anything could happen. Whenever my parents and I drove through the Lincoln Tunnel, I kept my eyes peeled for the tiled line in the tunnel wall indicating the border between New Jersey and New York and felt an almost electrical *ping* shoot up my spine when we crossed that line and entered Manhattan, the tunnel spitting us out onto Ninth Avenue, into a world which seemed rich with possibility. The city, for me, usually meant a treat: tickets to *The Nutcracker* at Lincoln Center, a visit to my grandmother's apartment on Central Park West, overlooking the steeples of the Dakota. A turkey, tongue, coleslaw, and Russian dressing sandwich at Fine & Schapiro on Seventy-second Street, where the old waitresses would treat my father like a boy, urging him to eat more, chucking him under the chin.

But inevitably, we would head home. I would sit in the backseat and watch the Manhattan skyline disappear around the bend, and a familiar heaviness would descend as we passed back over the tiled border to the jagged, graffiti-covered cliffs of Jersey City, the newly built Newark airport, the neon Budweiser eagle slowly flapping its wings over the Anheuser-Busch plant.

• • •

I'm hard-pressed here, pushing, searching for something positive and uplifting to write about the place where I grew up. After all, it is my own internal landscape, the place where my stories began, and thinking about it raises a moral question: Would I trade my own painful childhood for a happier one and not possess this material as a writer? Those years of childhood isolation are what have shaped my voice. There is no doubt in my mind that those years made me a writer, but they could just as easily have made me psychotic.

We had a hard time in Hillside. It was just one of those towns, a piece of bad luck, the wrong place to live. We were surrounded by families who were all more like one another than we were like them. Worst of all, we were Orthodox Jews. In a neighborhood that didn't take kindly to Jewish families to begin with, my parents arrived with their foreign customs, such as a wooden *succab*—a glorified shack—which we erected in the backyard each autumn to celebrate the old harvest days with shafts of wheat and bitter lemons. We had mezuzahs on all the doors, and we didn't drive on the Sabbath. We were kosher, in every sense of the word. Each Saturday morning, my father would don a dark suit and yarmulke and walk the mile or so to synagogue, past the houses of those who had thrown eggs and set fire to his lawn.

If asked, my father would have defined himself first and foremost as a Jew. Even before he was a husband, a father, a Wall Street businessman, he was an observant Jew. The traditions of orthodoxy were his roots, the bedrock of the family he came from, and though he was probably conflicted at times, he never rebelled, never ran away. For a while, he and my mother agreed to raise me Orthodox. Until I was thirteen, I went to a yeshiva in a nearby town, where I became fluent in Hebrew and learned to climb around in the intellectual branches of the Talmud. But while my classmates went home to neighborhoods and communities where there were other Orthodox Jewish families, in my mother's chocolate-brown Eldorado I reentered a neighborhood where it was a bad thing, an odd thing, to be a Jew. It was the beginning of my sense of not-belonging; an invisible wall had gone up between me and the rest of the world, and before I knew it, I was banging against it, trying to get out.

In those days, we had live-in housekeepers, though now, as a grown woman, I don't understand why. I was an only child, and my mother didn't work outside the house. What did she do all day? The house was spotless. These housekeepers, who never lasted more than a year or two, were from faraway islands: Jamaica, Trinidad, Martinique, Antigua. They wore white uniforms during the day, and at night they retreated to a small room in the basement, near the laundry room, where it was implicitly understood I should not bother them. I now think of this room, with its small window which overlooked the inside of the metal grate in the backyard, and remember sneaking in and seeing Bibles, crosses, pictures of Jesus Christ.

My mother fired one housekeeper for asking her where her horns were. When my mother asked her what she meant, the housekeeper said she had been told Jews had horns. She was gone the next day. The others, they had a hard time getting the hang of our strict dietary laws and religious customs.

The kitchen had two sinks, two dishwashers. Milk and meat were kept strictly separate. And this isn't counting Passover, with its whole other set of dishes and the traditional, ritualistic banishing of all bread crumbs throughout the house with a flashlight and a feather.

*Going home, going back home. Going home to visit my parents.* These are words my grown friends still utter, friends well into their thirties and forties with families and children of their own. I tried to stop thinking of 885 Revere Drive as home when I first left it to go to college, sixteen years ago. I was in the midst of a fairly violent rebellion against my parents, and I hated everything the house and neighborhood had come to stand for: the bourgeois suburbia of private tennis courts, heated swimming pools, new Cadillacs, prized sons who went to medical schools, and the prized daughters who married them. Though more Jewish families moved into the neighborhood over the years and the overt anti-Semitism faded into something more subtle than burning lawns, it was a place that never felt like home. I was furious at my parents for digging their heels in and staying in a neighborhood where we were second-class citizens, for not seeing the writing on the wall back when I was an infant. Why hadn't they packed up and moved back into the city? There, I imagined, we would have been one among many families just like us, a single cell in a larger organism. I longed for community. And of course I was rebelling against Orthodoxy itself: while my classmates were sneaking around smoking pot during high school, I thought God would strike me dead for eating bacon or driving on the Sabbath. When real rebellion finally did strike, it did so with the force of a small tornado. It didn't let up until I was well into my twenties.

I felt like a wanderer, rootless, in need of a home. I tried to make a home for myself wherever I went, even in my college dorm room, where I hung a floral sheet over the window and kept lighted, scented candles on my nightstand. I chose a college which was listed in a guide to colleges as a "haven for neurotic upper-middle-class artsy types who don't know where they fit in." I fit right in. Then, at nineteen, I married for the first time—*not* a medical student—and went about the business of playing house while still in college, picking out fresh flowers each week at an outdoor market on Columbus Avenue, giving dinner parties, planting trees in huge terra-cotta pots. I decided I was a grown woman, that I could skip certain developmental steps (like late adolescence) as if skipping over Boardwalk in a game of Monopoly.

Even though I stayed away from Revere Drive and tried to forge a life of my own, I always knew it was there, a house I had lived in so long that I could have found my way from attic to kitchen blindfolded. I still knew just how many steps it took to get up the front walk, how many stairs separated the basement from the first floor. I still heard the milk box clanking with fresh bottles every Tuesday morning and saw the gardener trimming the forsythia hedges on alternate Thursdays. I knew where to find my own initials, which I had carved deeply into an attic beam to ensure they would always be there. But most important, I knew I could go there if I were sick, tired, in need of care—and that my old room was there for me anytime I wanted it, with its pink shag carpeting and the Ben Shahn lithograph on the wall.

By twenty, I was divorced. A twenty-year-old divorcée is, or should be, an oxymoron. I felt too old to go back home and have my mother take care of me, and I was too embarrassed to return to dorm life, so I rented a cottage at the end of a long dirt road not far from college. Each night I'd stay awake into the early-morning hours with my golden retriever, listening to the creaks of the cottage, the wind howling through the trees. The cottage was on the property of a sculptor, a woman whose work took the form of huge plaster, metal, and concrete boulders that littered the fields around the house. If I peered out my window in the middle of the night, by the light of the moon those boulders looked like droppings from some nasty prehistoric creature—a grown-up version of the shadow on the wall, the monster in the closet.

I was accomplishing one part of my objective—putting distance between me and home—but my quest was beginning to have the unfortunate side effect of making me feel even more rootless than before. While I was in the throes of my rebellion, swimming against the current, something stronger than me was beginning to pull me back.


I often give my creative writing students this exercise: Write about a house from the point of view of a character who has just lost her child in a war; then describe the same house from the point of view of a character who has just fallen in love.

This exercise stumps them. When they return to class after a week of struggling, they are often frustrated, filled with questions: How do the actual physical properties of a place change, they wonder, depending on point of view? A wastebasket is a wastebasket, an oven is an oven.

The key to creating a sense of place lies with the narrator, I tell them. The details, in and of themselves, are not important. They are a reflection of the inner life of the teller of the story. And as we discuss the meaning of metaphor, I am drawn back to a moment in my own life, a moment in which I am a grown woman, sitting in my car outside my parents' house.

I am twenty-three, and my father has just died in a car crash, an accident that very nearly also took my mother's life. She is in the hospital, her legs shattered into eighty pieces. It is unclear whether she will walk again, whether she will recover from the immensity of this physical and emotional blow. After a lifetime spent protecting themselves from the world, my parents have had their lives busted wide open on a New Jersey highway.

Six months earlier, my parents had finally moved from the house at 885 Revere Drive. They were looking for a calmer, more aesthetically pleasing life for their later years, and a house in a more rural part of New Jersey was supposed to do the trick. I did not come home to help my parents move. When my mother called to ask what I wanted her to do with my wooden Russian dolls, the white Formica dresser with its orange knobs, the poster I kept on my bedroom wall—*If you have to get out of town, get in front of the crowd and make it look like a parade*—I told her she could throw it all away. I believed I had no sentimental attachment to the stuff of my childhood. It never occurred to me that my parents, both in their sixties at this point, might need my help moving out. Nor did I go see their new home. I was angry with them for moving because it made me realize what I had long known, that we could have moved many years earlier, perhaps to a more welcoming community.

So there I am, days after my father's death, sitting in my car. My mother has asked me to go to their house—the one I have never visited—to pick up the mail, throw out any spoiled food, check the pipes to make sure nothing is frozen. She gives me directions to the house, and I drive there early one winter afternoon.

I pull up to a newish, pale brick house on a hill, more bland than I had imagined. There is snow on the ground, and the driveway is unnegotiable. On my car radio I am listening to a Brahms piano concerto. I am alone, adrift, twenty-three. My lips and nose are chapped from two solid weeks of tears.

I park the car and make my way around to the back of the house, my boots leaving deep imprints on the snow covering the driveway. My breath is a cloud in front of me. My mother has told me to let myself in through the garage, and I do so, pressing the familiar alarm code, fiddling with strange, new keys. As the garage door slowly rises, I notice my father's green rubber galoshes on the floor, his tweed cap hanging on a hook.

Later that day, after spending the afternoon wafting through my parents' new house and sorting through mail addressed to a dead man, I lock up, turn on the various alarm systems, and begin to drive back to the city. But my car has a mind of its own, and as we reach Exit 14 on the Jersey Turnpike, I find myself signaling left, getting on the exit ramp, and driving down the icy streets until I am somehow parked in front of 885 Revere Drive.

The most obvious Freudian interpretation of a dream about a house is that the house symbolizes the unconscious—the deepest part of the self. I stare at the white columns of the house in which I spent the first eighteen years of my life, the front lawn blanketed with snow, the second-floor window where my bedroom used to be. There are lights glowing inside. This house contains my secrets—secrets which may never be fully excavated on an analyst's couch or in the unconscious metaphors of my fiction. I contemplate knocking on the door, ringing the bell which may or may not still chime eight times, and introducing myself to the stranger who answers. "I lived here once," I will say, and this fact will connect us, the way siblings separated at birth are connected by the realization that they share a parent. The house is my mother, a womb for my dreams, the place where a door to a hidden room might finally creak open, a wealth of dark jewels tumbling out.

I gaze at the second-floor bedroom window and remember a night when I was sixteen and my neighborhood friend, Allison, and I decided to sneak out of the house and go to a party around the corner. It was a party we were strictly forbidden to attend, given by the sons of the neighbors my parents had always suspected were the culprits behind the violence years earlier.

This time it is a balmy night in early spring. My parents are out, and my cousin Sylvia is babysitting. Along with three alarm systems and babysitters for sixteen-year-olds, my parents believed in the additional preventative measure of a folding chain-link ladder which was kept on the top shelf of the closet in my second-floor bedroom.

Allison and I, dressed in our best light blue corduroys, Docksiders, and Lacoste alligator shirts, drag the ladder from its storage place and hook it over the sill of my window, peering down to the flagstone patio below. It looks like a long way down. We lower the ladder, careful not to let it clang against the side of the house, particularly not against the shutters of the living room where Sylvia sits on the real couch, listening to *La Traviata* on an enormous stereo system with two globe-like speakers.

Across the lawn, rock 'n' roll is drifting our way. The neighborhood boys are considerably older than Allison and me, old enough to have driver's licenses and kegs of beer. Their friends' Volkswagen beetles and ten-year-old Volvos are parked all the way down the street. It is so glamorous to me. I pat my pants pocket, making sure I have my soft pack of Marlboro Reds, hoist myself over the window ledge, and start to straddle the window—when Sylvia's head pokes out the front door.

When my parents got home that night, Sylvia handed us over like two collared dogs. I was grounded for a couple of days; Allison wasn't allowed to accompany me to summer camp because, according to her parents, I was a "bad influence."

· · ·

Later that summer, I wound up making out with one of those sons. I knew that he and his parents probably still called us dirty Jews behind our backs, that they had tried to burn us out of the neighborhood when I was a child. He invited me into his house, up to his room, where he still lived with his parents at the age of twenty-eight. I felt like a secret agent; I had snuck behind enemy lines. I knew I was doing the *very worst thing* I could possibly do, which was exactly why I was doing it. I was very blond and blue-eyed and had been fielding comments—compliments!—about how much I looked like a shiksa, a non-Jewish woman. I wondered, as he kissed me and I felt his full beard scratch my lips, my cheeks, why I was good enough for him to kiss but not good enough to live nearby. I let him put his hands on my breasts. I kept my eyes open the whole time, watching his desire grow, feeling him get hard against my thigh as we rolled around on his single bed beneath the football pennants he had won a decade earlier. His eyes were a cold, icy blue.

As I sit in my car with the engine idling, I stare hard at the front lawn of 885 Revere Drive until the snow begins to shift, an avalanche of memory. I see a girl and her mother walking hand in hand through the snow, dragging a sled behind them. I see a blond child in a white snowsuit, building a snowman with a carrot for a nose and Oreo cookies for eyes. I squint and imagine my father pulling into the driveway in his ancient Citroën, his galoshes on his feet and his tweed cap covering his bald head.

I light a cigarette—a few years later I will quit—and walk

around the side of the house. The pool, which my parents installed after my father's back surgery so he could do laps, is covered by a dark green tarp, and a small wooden bird feeder in the shape of a house hangs from the lowest bare branch of the elm near the kitchen window. A wood-paneled station wagon is parked in the driveway, and I dully remember my parents telling me that the new owners have several kids.

I wonder if the house is cursed—whether in the proportion of the rooms, the angle of the roof, the rise of the chimney, there is an unwritten code which will bring any family who lives here unhappiness. At twenty-three, I am confused as my future students will some day be confused—I am bestowing power on the inanimate, giving objects independent meaning of their own. My father is dead, my mother is in traction, and I am a baby-divorcée who smokes too much and has no idea what to do with her life. This house, with its redbrick facade and flagstone patio, is the container of a new family's joys and sorrows. But the darkness it holds for me remains carved into the beams of its attic, just like the initials I left behind.

# OGLING THE STATUE OF LIBERTY

## GAIUTRA BAHADUR

EXIT 14B

The source of the obscenities was a burly white man, the driver of a van parked near us.

"You Indians!" he roared. "You think you're so smart, but you're so fucking stupid! Yeah, bitch. You!"

We were waiting for my mother at the Journal Square Kiss and Ride, where the trains from Manhattan empty their cargo of commuters into the squat landscape of my home-town.

"Shut the fuck up."

My reply came from a raw, uncharted place. It surprised

even me. The driver sprang from his seat, walked over to our car and shoved his head into the window.

"What did you say?"

I collected my rage into a prim and proper sentence, perhaps more in keeping with his image of a brown-skinned girl in glasses: "One should treat people with dignity," I said. "It is the mark of intelligence."

He spat at us and walked off, cackling.

I grew up in a city where the flat-roofed row houses lean close together, ogling the backside of the Statue of Liberty like a cluster of lewd old men. I did my growing up there at the same time that racists were acting out against people who looked like me. I never blamed the city. In fact, I felt the same fighter's pride for it as I did for my family and for myself in its clutch of concrete and clapboard.

Jersey City became ours by default on November 8, 1981, the day we came to America.

I remember the ride from JFK Airport to our new home across the Hudson River. In particular, I remember looking up at two buildings the color and mood of silos. The Jersey City Medical Center seemed impossibly grand to my six-year-old eyes, but there is reason for their stature in my memory. They were our ticket to America. The nursing shortage of the 1970s brought the relatives who ultimately sponsored us as immigrants. They came to work the emergency rooms of the hospital, and they still do.

E. L. Doctorow once described Jersey City as "a dreary afterthought of New York, where the people all had that look of being no place."

It would have been more accurate to say that the people, or many of them anyhow, have that look of being from someplace else. Someplace foreign.

That has always been the case in Jersey City. It has always been a bootstrap place, where people go to begin again with nothing. Its view of the shining skyscrapers of New York, basking almost like a sixth borough in their reflected glow, probably had something to do with it.

At the last century's start, Jersey City's immigrants came from Ireland, Italy, and eastern Europe. In the last twenty-five years, they've arrived mainly from Asia, Latin America, the Middle East, and the West Indies. More than a third of its quarter million denizens were born outside this country.

The city forced all those layers into tight proximity.

Our house on Cambridge Avenue, a red flattop previously occupied by an elderly white widow, was hemmed in on three sides. Next door, Brenda Martinez regularly blasted Menudo. To the left lived an old couple whose Italian immigrant ancestors had preceded us by generations on the Palisades above the Hudson River. The pizzeria behind us gave up a constant clatter of plates and voices from its back kitchen. A chink between the houses to the rear revealed a sign for FANZETTI INSURANCE, the neon bulbs for the "R" smashed. Its busted-up glow at night gave romance to our hub of working-class respectability, a section of the city called the Heights.

Not everyone was happy with its polyglot character, however. In 1987, the same year we moved to our very own house, bigots began terrorizing the neighborhood. We picked up the local broadsheet to find their crudely scrawled manifesto, signed "The Dotbusters": "We will go to any extreme to get Indians to move out of Jersey City," it read. "If I'm walking down the street and I see a Hindu and the setting is right, I will hit him or her."

They weren't bluffing. Three white men armed with baseball bats beat an Indian doctor so severely he later couldn't remember enough to lock them up. The attack took place blocks from our house, and my parents wouldn't let us play outside that fall. A man in a car that had stopped next to ours at a red light spat directly into my father's face. Another time, hoodlums brandishing broken bottles chased him for blocks. Someone scrawled "Hindus Go Home" in black paint across the side of our house, and my mother spent the next day scouring the aluminum siding with paint thinner.

Jersey City's Indian enclave, overflow from New York like most of its lifeblood and most of its immigrants, is riotous. Indian flags flap from the lampposts in a tattered row of saffron, green, and white. Posters gaudy with color and melodrama advertise masala musicals, and songs from those flicks spill onto the street from video stores, thick like the smell of cumin. We—living in the orbit of Gandhi Square with its clutter of curry and sari shacks—looked like we were a part of it all.

We weren't, exactly. My family immigrated from Guyana, a sugarcane republic in South America about the size and shape of New Jersey, with a population less than one eighth as large. The British, who once ruled the country, imported shiploads of indentured Indians to replace slaves on their plantations there in the nineteenth century. We are their descendants, doubly displaced.

Hate crime did tighten up the screws of solidarity that England had already put in, somewhat loosely, over the course of building an empire. But my parents did not make new friends because of the hooligans who terrorized the Indian and the Indian-looking in the Heights. In fact, they did not have many friends at all. They continued to turn inward, and except for the constant intimacy of so many uncles, aunts, and cousins, our home became a fortress.

Outside, after all, there lurked physical threat.

But America in its accents and its habits also lay there. Outside defined *normal*. For one, everybody knew girls have boyfriends, go to proms, grow up to move away and own their own lives.

Inside, my immigrant parents knew no such thing because, inside, an elsewhere continued to exert its influence. If the tens of thousands of foreigners who lived in Jersey City were at all like us, then ours was—is—a city of people cleaved in two by the front door.


My childhood in New Jersey unfolded mostly indoors. We lived for our first six American years in rented rooms in my uncle's house. From the fire escape, beyond his garden of vegetables transplanted from Guyana, you could see the Twin Towers.

Despite the wide-open view, our apartment promoted claustrophobia.

My mother used to sit on the edge of the bathtub, her hands attacking the clothes in the sudsy water. The door swung into the windowless bathroom to reveal her bent that way, pummeling hand-me-down jeans until they screeched, beating the ugly green corduroys that made me look as awkward as I felt, scrubbing, wringing and generally doing battle. She nearly fainted once, with the fumes of Clorox concentrated in that little room. It made the inside lining of her nostrils burn. It made her eyeballs sting. It found its way deep down into her throat and made her gag.

It didn't help that my remembrances of the era B.A., or Before America, were all set outdoors.


The houses in the villages that dot the Guyanese coast stand on stilts. That kicks opens a whole terrain underneath called the Bottom House, where hammocks are slung, vegetables are cut, babies and laundry are washed, gossip is exchanged, and rum and Coke rules masculine evenings.

There was a Hindu temple the size of a toolshed in our front yard. It was honeycombed with holes for ventilation and painted as improbably blue as the gods within. The temple sat next to my grandmother's garden, where so many times, zinnias tucked into our braids, my cousin and I played at being brides. My cousin the taxi driver parked his curvaceous blue car at the front gate when it died, and its rusted fender still sits there today, in the weeds choking our abandoned plot of Guyanese earth.

The temple, the garden, and the car make up the hazy geography of that first childhood, like Colorforms stickers pasted onto a map of the past. They represented what was, in a place left behind. However flat they might have been, they were bright and vivid.

The close spaces of our new life in America collaborated to keep Memory locked in with the rest of us, like an extra family member who had a bad habit of constantly comparing things—and people—to the way they used to be.

In Guyana, my father was a god to me. He came home every weekend from university in the capital city bearing fudge. (I called it "fub.") Later he drove me to Teacher Annie's Preschool on his motorcycle, his arms protecting me between the handlebars. In those days, he posed for a picture in front of the temple in full swagger, his right hand hanging jauntily from its gate. I always did have a hard time believing in that young man, with the handsome arrogance of his smile and the effortless sense of belonging in his bearing.

America transformed my father. He started off by hauling boxes at a Rickel Home Center off a highway somewhere. He went to school in the evenings, since a degree from the University of Guyana meant nothing here. And he drank, too much.

My mother worked too, as a clerk in the Garment District in Manhattan. No need there for her Latin or French or her ability to recite "The Prisoner of Chillon" word for word.

My hot-item parents—shining in their youth and good looks, the "it" couple when they met as teachers back home—were now immigrants of the beaten-down variety well known in the literature of becoming American. They fought, sometimes bitterly.

Our aunts gave me and my cousin matching gray winter

coats. We wore them through our first season of snow. We learned how to speak and shoved indoors the Creole words that vibrated with Bottom House and playmates, altercation and intimacy, mother and father. There wasn't a whole lot of room for those words: we lived in three tight rooms, and we slept five in a row, on two beds pushed together, for half a decade.

The gods, too, were crowded. They too had been forced inside. From the airy temple perfumed by zinnias, they were driven into the closet—the linen closet in the bedroom, to be precise.

There was a box of Barbie dolls on the bottom shelf, and nightly, the rats made incisions into the pale plastic of their perfectly formed legs. On the top shelf rested the framed pictures of the gods: elephant-trunked Ganesh, the remover of obstacles; Hanuman, the monkey with a mountain in his palm; and Sarasvati, the goddess of knowledge.

Every Sunday, the white shutters of the linen closet would open; fresh flowers were placed on a bronze plate and incense sticks lit. My mother would sing bhajans, or the hymns of the Hindu holy books. She knows very little Hindi. Yet there was always in her cadence—in that lovely, high voice— a crack of sadness seducing me into false belief.

"I have occupied the insides of every last syllable of this song," said that crack in her voice.

Sundays always began with my mother's prayers resonating through the barely awake hallways. She intoned, *"Main ik nanha sa, main ik chota sa, baccha hoon,"* with an undercurrent of ache in her voice. (The words mean "I am a tiny, I am a small child.")

She stood in front of the makeshift altar with a white lace

scarf over her head, and she prayed with her eyes shut so tightly they could almost blot out racist graffiti and the world of threat and change outside her home.

Those early years in Jersey City often sent my twenty-something-year-old mother to her shuttered gods. And they gave her hymns a tangible quality.

*"Main ik nanha sa, main ik chota sa, baccha hoon."*

You could touch the words. They bent down to your feet, imploring your blessings: "I am tiny, I am a small child."

To me, the past was a better place because my parents were whole there. Maybe, when my mother prayed, she was still there, with the man mugging in front of the temple.

Jersey City, fiercely the present, was the place where my parents seemed to come apart, and it was the place where my own psyche split in two.

I remember sitting on the edge of the bed once, playing with the straps on my sneakers. It was some obscene hour of the morning, and we were going to see our cousins off on a visit to Guyana. My memory of this is distinct. The straps were Velcro, and I was in a sour mood.

That changed when I saw Kumar Gaurav's face fill the screen of our black-and-white Zenith, tuned to a station that broadcast Hindi film songs on Sunday mornings.

It was a scene from *Love Story*, a Bollywood musical I had last seen at a cinema hall in the capital of our province in Guyana. The hero, a Romeo repackaged for the subcontinent, was haunting the grounds of his Juliet's home on the day of her wedding to someone else. His chiseled face was long and soulful, and his star-crossed song seduced her through the static of the Zenith.

It's not that I was a Kumar Gaurav groupie, though at nine years old, I might incidentally have been. I used to have dreams then of waking up in our village from forever-long stays in a Nighttown made up of three claustrophobic rooms, a Zenith TV set, and a linen closet hiding Technicolor deities. America was a dream I kept waking up from, in my dreams. At that time, the scene from *Love Story* had the warm glow of a flashback to Guyana, like cod-liver oil or Marmite or an overheard snippet of Creolese on the otherwise ordinary street. All were part of the ghettoes of most-at-homeness in a world that was slowly becoming double.

Outside, the Americans were speaking Proper English. Inside were all the secrets, good and bad: the broken English, the dal and roti on Sunday mornings and the lachrymose lyrics of Lata Mangeshkar. (The GOLden VOICE of BOLLYwood, the men who gave us our cassette culture kept telling us.)

Entrenched inside, my mother kept throwing up ramparts, building up a fortress of "Who We Are," which we all had, nonetheless, to leave for hours at a time every day.

We left it for a city that, when it wasn't spitting in our face, sympathized. We weren't alone. Others, too, had mothers who did battle with dirty clothes and the tensions of reinvention in a completely alien landscape. I may not have belonged in Jersey City, but neither did most of my classmates. Mohamed Ibrahim, Jeannie Wong, Taras Ferencevych, Nancy Garcia, Rahul Reddy—each of us was an immigrant child or the child of immigrants, and each of us was cleaved in two by the front door.

The city was as scrappy and rough-edged as we were. Once a hub for factories, it had lost five thousand jobs in the six years before we came to America. It had hemorrhaged many more residents for three decades. Its housing stock was brittle and blighted. The public schools were so troubled the state had to take them over.

Alexander Solzhenitsyn, the Russian poet, spent part of his exile in Jersey City. The Egyptian cleric accused of plotting the first World Trade Center bombing, Sheikh Omar Abdel Rahman, preached at a storefront mosque steps away from Journal Square. The city's other semicelebrities had included Frank Hague, a political boss who ruled with an iron fist for three decades. The textbooks, when they talked about corruption in this era, mentioned Tammany Hall. And they mentioned Hague.

The Jersey City beyond our threshold was awash in escapes, plots, scandal, and failure. Was it any wonder my mother tried to cloister us? Despite the city's dubious claims to fame, I loved it. I loved the city in spite of itself. I loved it the way you love an underdog, with a rooting, irrational zeal that overlooks flaws.

Jersey City, after all, tried to lay claim to the Statue of Liberty. It attempted to wrest her from New York in a battle that went all the way to the Supreme Court. It didn't matter that Jersey City lost. It had demonstrated daring. It wanted to be somebody. Not only did it want to get out of the shadow of New York, it proposed to take a symbolic landmark from its neighbor across the river. This bravado was not unlike our own burning row house ambition, and it makes me love the city even more intensely.

I cannot blame it for being the scene of our loss and longing for an ever-more-distant homeland. Just as I cannot blame it for the xenophobes armed with spray paint and spittle, or the toll that emigrating took on our psyches.

Slowly, over the years, inside and outside have begun to bleed into each other. We have asserted ourselves in the outside world: when my grandmother died, we scattered her ashes in the Hudson River. Not Canje Creek, near our village in Guyana; nor the Ganges. And the outside world, of course, stole in past the ramparts of our house long ago. There have been boyfriends, and three daughters who moved away to own their own lives.

The world outside became a little less menacing as well. The Dotbusters, conjured in a note to a newspaper, seemed to vanish as an organized group not long after. Of course, there were still lone jerks who spewed hatred, just as there is still latent hostility to foreigners in Jersey City. The targets, since September 11, 2001, have widened especially to include Muslims and Arabs.

My parents live now in a house too big for just the two of them in a suburb near Newark. Now they have their American Dream: the white picket fence, the fireplace with sitcom-style family portrait hung above and ridiculous grass for my father to mow every Sunday.

He takes pride in having the grass to mow. Sometimes I watch him struggle with the expanse of it. He mows after Bacardi and Coke has dulled the edges of the day. By then the drink has usually brought out the dialect of a place before

Proper English. He stops from time to time, his glasses sliding down the bridge of his nose, and looks around self-consciously. I watch the middle-aged man behind the mower in New Jersey, trying so hard to look crisp and comfortable, and sometimes I see the ghost of that young man in front of the garden temple in Guyana.

# THE COMMUTE

## (Hoboken, 1996)

## CHRISTIAN BAUMAN

EXIT 14C

I f commute you must—and hey, eight million a day do—going home nights on the PATH train from World Trade Center to Hoboken isn't too brutal. Crowded, all right, this time of day. Packed so you can't move, sure. But that's New Jersey; it's all relative. There are longer commutes, deadlier rides home. NJ Transit to Trenton; good God. Driving the GWB to Fort Lee and I-80 beyond; have mercy. The PATH; well, pay your buck, what the fuck. It's just under the river.

You don't even try to find a seat, this time of day. Slip in the door, sidle over, grab the overhead rail. It's all slamming elbows and assholes, but less than fifteen minutes, who cares. Don't breathe too hard and steer clear of the sneezers. Actual illness leads to a waste of valuable sick time, sweet precious sick time, and you can get sick on the PATH this time of year, you bet you can. Hold your breath, hold the rail, and hang on those fifteen minutes.

The PATH, she rolls back and forth, back and forth, picking up that dark and weightless underground speed, steadying out the faster she goes. PATH doesn't rattle like the NYC subway, she rolls. Her cars are cleaner, too. That's something, anyway.

"*Ho*boken, laststopHoboken." Then again as she pulls into the old blue-tile underground station. "*Ho*bokenstation. *Ho*boken."

Two things born in Hoboken, New Jersey (hardly the only two things, but a good representation, as good a place as any to start), the memory of both births enshrined almost randomly on steel signs scattered like jacks across the mile-square city: the game of baseball and Francis Albert Sinatra. The former birth disputed by a small, insignificant, yet surprisingly powerful burg in upstate New York; the later birth disputed by none yet mostly spurned by the birthee himself.

"*Ho*bokenstation, laststop, leddemoff first, leddemoff first, leddemoff first—Ho*bo*ken."

Crowded, the commute. Packed. But late nights—that's a better story: the late-night station, waiting in a silent hollow echo and drip drip dripping from the tunnel cave beyond the platform; ten minutes, twenty minutes, lean back in the shadows and wait. She comes with a wait, but late nights the PATH train is a shiny railed limo. Empty and spacious, your smooth, cheap cruise below the Hudson. Couples coupling sometimes in the back car, deep kisses, furtive glances. Never a cop on the PATH, so it's just whether you care what a fellow rider sees.

"I got laid on the PATH last night," one overheard young suit tells another.

"Laid?"

"Well. Close to it."

"You put the 'ho' in Hoboken, my friend."

A pause, then "I think that's the sweetest thing anyone's ever said to me."

But not evening rush hour, no. Not the commute. The commute, we're all fish in the stream. Pushing and rubbing and pressing in all the wrong ways.

"Leddemoff first, leddemoff first—*Ho*bokenstationlast-stop."

From the inside out, then; released from the open doors of the PATH train and packed up the stairs to the street. Follow slow, if you're smart, hands in overcoat pockets and head up. Rise from the train. Allow the world to flow around you. A smooth stone in a rushing eddy, all that torrent racing by, rising up to Hoboken. Slide by, unaffected; take her slow into Hoboken and rise.

## HELL, HOME, OR HOBOKEN

### CAROLINE LEAVITT

EXIT 14C

## Hoboken, 1993

It's 98 degrees out and I'm two weeks past the delivery date of my first child, worrying about the three days left I have before the hospital will induce me. The only thing taking my mind off my swollen belly and my discomfort and fear is the Saint Anne's festival booming down my block.

I'm Jewish and I don't know anything about Saint Anne except that everyone here seems just crazy about her. They can't wait to see her statue, to touch it. The whole street is alive with noise and firecrackers and the shiny blast of trombones and whistles. People are tumbling out of their houses to watch and listen and clap one another on the back in the sheer delight of the day. Someone is passing out zeppole, special pastries that are warm and dusted with powdered sugar, served in paper bags cloudy with extra sugar, and if I weren't feeling so wobbly, I'd have one, too. The streets are lined with people, the street is crowded with marching bands, and men are wearing suits and kids are in their Sunday best. Every once in a while someone turns to nod at me as I lean, exhausted and huge, in my doorway. Ten beefy men hoist up a huge statue of a robed woman, covered with dollar bills, and the woman beside me grabs my arm and shouts into my ear, "It's Saint Anne, honey! Go and put a dollar on her and you'll have a healthy baby!" I blink at her. "Go on," she urges, giving me a gentle prod. "It's good luck. She's the patron saint of women." She ferrets in her pocket and pulls out a dollar and folds it into my hand, and because this is my first pregnancy and my first year in my new Hoboken neighborhood, I make my way into the thickening crowd, which parts for me. Hands guide me to Saint Anne. "Let the pregnant lady through!" someone calls, and then I'm there, by the statue, which is chipped and sticky with tape and covered with dollar bills, and other hands guide me to put my dollar on the statue, too.

"Saint Anne, Saint Anne, bring me a man!" screams a young girl, and I look at my belly and think: *It's a boy,* and I put up the dollar. When I make my way back, one of my neighbors hugs me.

Seven hours later, I go into labor and have my son.

# 1980

Before I ever lived in Hoboken, I lived in Boston. Born and bred there, I loved the hum and snap of the city and even went to college at Brandeis because I couldn't bear to leave town. I admit I liked, too, telling people I was from Boston. It sounded cool. It *was* cool. And by association, so was I. Right up until I began meeting more and more people at Brandeis who were from Manhattan, who had a mystique about them that overpowered my own. They lived in a city that didn't shut down at 2 A.M. the way Boston did but was open all night. Their museums and music joints and restaurants all made Boston's seem a little—well—freshly scrubbed and unadventurous.

And so, eventually, I heeded Manhattan's siren song, and I moved there, and as soon as I did, I knew I would never leave, because what place on Earth could possibly be better? I loved meeting my friends for pie at four in the morning at the Empire Diner. I adored my tiny Chelsea apartment, just big enough to contain my all-black wardrobe. Any chance I could slide it into the conversation, I made sure to mention that I was a New Yorker. I lived there happily for fifteen years, right through the 1980s, and I would have stayed there forever, but then I fell in love with Jeff, another writer. Since his New York City apartment was even crummier than mine (I had neighbors who wore leather and whipped each other. All night we could hear the crack of that whip, the shrieks and moans. Staying at Jeff's apartment was no better. Jeff's neighbors kept a rooster who crowed him awake every morning at five), we knew we had to find a place. We knew we each needed a home office to write in. We knew we wanted a child. And we knew we could no more afford that in Manhattan than we could afford to buy a small country.

Desperate, we looked in Brooklyn, which was a forty-five-minute subway ride away. We looked way uptown in Manhattan, which was even longer, and then Jeff suggested New Jersey, which deeply offended my New York sensibilities. New Jersey! That was what we New Yorkers called "bridge-and-tunnel" people, because those were the structures they had to use to get to the promised land of Manhattan. I hadn't left Boston for New York only to have to leave New York for . . . New Jersey.

"Come on," I said. "New Jersey's a punch line. We can't live in a joke."

"We can live in Hoboken," he assured me.

We knew the stories. Hoboken in the '80s was a dump, but it was an affordable dump. One single square mile of real estate. Manhattan pioneers were fleeing their expensive rents to grab up the gorgeous turn-of-the-century Hoboken brownstones. To help this conversion along, landlords raised the rents so high they priced people out of their homes and businesses, and when that didn't work, they used threats and bullying, and then a sudden, terrifying spate of arson erupted. People died or became homeless; they left in despair or disgust. And then the newcomers came in, people with money enough to gut the old houses, remodel them, and then sell them for a profit, usually to someone who would do the exact same thing. Very few people gave to the community or respected it. Was it any wonder the old-time Hobokenites began to hate and distrust the new?

We got off the subway ("Just seven minutes and one stop from the heart of the Village!" Jeff said), and I pulled the collar of my leather jacket up and slunk so that it covered half my face. I squinted, trying to close out as much of Hoboken as I could, but when I saw the beautiful old brownstones, the cobblestones by the waterfront, I began to take a closer look. We roamed past shops and restaurants and a few cafés. Okay, I admitted. It was sort of urban, it had a buzz, but definitely at a lower speed than Manhattan. We passed two bookstores and a movie theater with a double feature of two indie movies I wanted to see. "Come on. What more do we need?" Jeff asked.

"Manhattan?" I said. Just yesterday a friend had told me that we were leaving civilization. Another friend had helpfully suggested we look in Queens; then we could still say we lived in Manhattan. "You don't really want to be a Jersey Girl, do you?" asked another friend, and she said "Jersey" as if it were an incurable disease.


On our way to the realtor, I picked up the local journal, the *Hoboken Reporter,* and stared, dumbfounded, at the letters. Three whole pages of vitriol against the new people who were moving into the town. These newcomers, these Manhattan expatriates, had no respect for Hoboken culture. Worse, they had no curtains on their windows. They listened to disgusting chamber music. "Go home!" one writer cried. "We don't want you or your ways here! Go home!" I folded the paper over and quietly looked at Jeff. "They want us to go home," I said.

"Maybe we are home," Jeff said calmly.

We looked at thirty houses that day, brownstones and brick town houses that dated back to the 1860s, and to my amazement, they were ten times the size of our apartments. They had three floors and huge bay windows, and some even had little wooded backyards with decks and gardens. There were eat-in kitchens and living rooms and decks, and astonishingly, we could afford all of it. We stood in the middle of a house that needed work. Built in 1865, it was covered in cheap wood paneling and orange shag, but two rooms on the second floor had marble fireplaces, and one room had moldings on the ceiling and a rosette, and all I could think was: *I could love it here.*

I looked at Jeff's bright, expectant face. "Let's buy it," I said. The day the papers were signed, we tore down the wood paneling. Behind it were fireplaces. We tore up the rugs to find wide plank oak floors. Under the lowered ceiling were turn-of-the-century brass chandeliers. My mouth dropped open. I hugged Jeff. "Told you," he said happily.

We moved into a house that was a work in progress. We hired a team of contractors, who blithely told us our wiring and plumbing were below code and would have to be totally replaced, and oh yes, so was our deck. And let's not even talk about the roof yet.

We were too involved with renovations to really think about what it felt like to live in Hoboken. We tried to do our work in the one room that wasn't being worked on, and we ran to the local café for lunch and dinner. Our neighbors were nowhere to be found. "Don't worry," our contractor told us. "I've done houses around here, and I can tell you, Hobokenites are the nosiest people on Earth. By now, they know all about you, right down to what brand of dish detergent you like."

We laughed, but two days later, when the contractors were out buying supplies, I heard a noise downstairs, a whistling, and I went down to find a strange man, idly looking around the house.

"Can I help you?" I asked, alarmed. He looked at the wood floors we had revealed. "The Custers liked carpeting," he said.

"Can I help you?" I repeated.

He thrust out his hand. "Why, I'm Mick. I live down the block. I wanted to see what you're doing here." He nodded at me. "You must be Caroline, right?"

I started. He knew my name and Jeff's. He knew where we had come from and what our jobs were. "You can make a living as writers?" he said. He didn't like that we had torn down the paneling to reveal fireplaces. ("We cemented ours up," he said. "More economical. The smart thing to do.") And he didn't like that we didn't have Christmas decorations up.

"We're Jewish," I told him.

He studied me, frowning, silent for a moment. "So?" he said, finally. "You could still put up decorations. Five years ago every house on this block was all lit up for Christmas. *Every* house," he said. "Put up Jewish stars, then. Just decorate."

I tried to guide him to the door. "Thank you for coming over," I said pointedly. He ran one hand down the beautiful old fireplace we had uncovered. "We hope you're not going to change too much," he said, and then he was gone. I locked the door after him.

We began to see more and more of the neighbors. Bert and his wife, Eddie, gave us a coffee cake and then told us how unhappy they were that we had taken down the short wire fence in our backyard and replaced it with a high wood one.

"No one has fences like that," said Bert. "How're you going to talk to your neighbors that way?"

"No one has them," he repeated, and his voice began to sound like a snarl.

"I guess we do," Jeff said.

"And another thing," Bert said. "I don't like the work you're doing on your front steps. My railing's on there."

"I thought it was a shared railing."

"Not anymore," he said, and left.

A week later we got a letter from his lawyer. Bert's railing was on our property, and he wanted it back. We had our contractor remove the railing and move it two inches over so it was Bert's again. After that, Bert never spoke to us but whistled loudly when we passed. His wife, Eddie, always smiled and was friendly, but only when she was by herself. When she was with Bert, she glanced down at the ground.

We got complaints when we sandblasted off the thick gray paint on our house, revealing beautiful old brick. We got an angry letter when we called the police, concerned over the firecrackers and minibombs a neighbor was setting off by the phone lines and the wires one New Year's Eve. "We've been doing this for years!" he shouted at us. "You come along, and now we have to stop!"

"Great," I said to Jeff. "We have a house we love and neighbors who hate us."

I got pregnant that spring. I bought a dress to show off my speed bump of a belly and took a walk on Willow Street. I was coming back home when I ran into Emma. She studied me for a moment. "You're pregnant?" she asked, and I nodded, shy and pleased. "Our first!" I said.

"So you'll be moving soon," she said, resigned.

"Moving? We aren't going anywhere. We love it here."

She frowned, puzzled. "You're not going to where you think the schools are better?"

I shook my head.

"You're staying? You're really staying?"

"Of course we're staying."

"No one stays," she said, marveling. "They zip off to the suburbs. Our schools aren't good enough for them. Our town isn't good enough for them."

A tiny little woman dressed in black, a black kerchief about her head, stared at my belly, crossed herself and spat in my path. I flinched, but Emma linked her arm in mine. "She's doing that for good luck," she explained.

Another neighbor walked by. "Betty!" Emma called. "They're staying." Emma pointed to my belly. "And she's pregnant!"

Betty grinned. "I have a coffee cake. Both of you come over and help me eat it."

•    •    •

After that, things changed. It was nearing spring, and the neighbors pulled out plastic lawn chairs and set them up in front of their homes in the evenings and talked. They shared pitchers of lemonade and kids played in the nearly empty streets, and when they saw Jeff and me walking, they hailed us over. "Sit!" commanded a neighbor on one side of me. They wanted to know everything. Where was I giving birth? Who was my doctor? "Manhattan?" one neighbor said. "Why can't you deliver at St. Mary's? It's two blocks away. Who's your doctor, maybe I know a better one."

"Stop being so nosy," someone said.

But it didn't feel like noisiness to me. It felt like concern, and I was happy to have it.

I got sick after I had my first child. I was in a coma for two weeks, in the hospital for two months, and sick for a year. And the neighbors were incredible. We found casseroles on our doorstep. They offered to help out. They cheered me when I learned to walk again, and they cheered my son as well. We began to be included in the evening talks out on the stoops. I got well. I wrote and published a novel, and when I had a reading at Barnes & Noble, all the neighbors came. All of them bought a book.

On 9/11, my son saw the towers burn from his kindergarten window. Together, we watched them fall from the Hudson. Hoboken became an emergency zone. For weeks afterward the air had a metallic, horrible smell. Posters were everywhere. *Missing. Missing. Missing.* It didn't matter where you lived, New York or Hoboken. We were all in this together, all under siege. I thought of a line from that old Joni Mitchell song, about not knowing what you've got until it's gone, and I realized, more than I ever had, how much I loved Hoboken.

We donated money, we gave blood, we were dazed. This was, more than ever, our home.

It's 2006 now, and when I think of Manhattan, it's like the city's an old lover.

People want to live in Hoboken now! Last week, a Manhattan friend called me, asking if I knew of any houses for sale in Hoboken. When we first moved to Hoboken, there were more than thirty of them. Now, leafing through the local paper for my friend, I find two, and both are the cost of a space flight to Mars. That evening, I see a realtor showing a young couple the house across the street.

I hear the couple talking with the realtor, about our last mayor, who was indicted and is now serving jail time. About our new mayor, who has gentrified the city so much that many people can't afford to live here anymore. They ask about the Saint Anne festival, the rockets and fireworks that still go off, and the realtor guides the conversation into Hoboken's new parks and waterfronts, the new skating rink and swimming pool and arts center, the four-star restaurants and chic little shops.

The couple step back and study the house, and then the man whispers something to the woman. "We'll gut it," says the woman, excitedly, and all I keep thinking is, are they going to stay? Will they be good neighbors?

I wait until the couple leaves, and then I start walking to the ends of the town. I heard on the news that a local eccentric, who's kept a Jesus shrine for years, suddenly proclaimed that the statue of Jesus opened its eye. It was a miracle! People are flocking to see it, to imagine they might be helped or healed or simply nurtured by the sight. I don't know what I expect as I walk to see it, what I think might occur in yet another one of Hoboken's religious happenings.

I turn down another street, and there's the statue that everyone is coming to see. It looks like an ordinary Jesus. Maybe a little paint has flaked from one eye. Maybe that's why people think it looks opened. I stare critically at the Jesus and I remember the first time I ever put a dollar on Saint Anne's robe, the year I was pregnant and had first moved here. Back then, I had felt like a stranger to Hoboken. Now, though, what I feel is something very different.

I glance closer at the Jesus statue. I swear it winks.

# UNCOMMON CRIMINAL

## JAMES KAPLAN

EXIT 145

L ongy Zwillman killed himself just a month before I arrived in the Oranges, not that it would have mattered much to me: I was seven at the time. Zwillman was fifty-five or thereabouts, though he could easily have passed for seventy—he'd always been ahead of his years—a sad, tired, sick old man of fifty-five, living on pills for high blood pressure, insomnia, anxiety, depression, constipation, what have you. Beyond a certain point life is barely worth living. Longy—real first name Abner—was a gangster, as you might have surmised or dimly recollected. And though he was a gangster of a rather unusual sort—a quiet and cultivated man, from all appearances, who loathed publicity and had forsworn a violent past—the federal government, especially in the person of John Edgar Hoover—demioctoroon, closet queen, Upholder of Christian Values—had always considered him just another hoodlum, and a Jew hoodlum to boot, certainly not a credit to his race. At the beginning of 1959, the FBI and the IRS, which had been watching Zwillman minutely for decades, hoping for him to make a slipup, were finally closing in, having just arrested a close associate for bribing two jurors in Zwillman's tax evasion trial several years before.

For twenty years, Zwillman had protected himself with a kind of Chinese wall, engaging (quite successfully) in a number of legitimate businesses and paying his taxes on them, always having the illegal work—the loan-sharking and bookmaking, the squeezing of the Newark window washers' union or the movie projectionists' union or the department store workers' union—handled by associates, or associates of associates. Besides the obvious practicality of the strategy, there was a kind of high-handedness to it, as though Longy couldn't bear to sully his hands. In fact, his business life was desperately strange: If he could succeed legitimately, after all, why persist in endangering himself with numbers running, with an illegal jukebox monopoly? Was it for the thrill, or was he driven by a compulsion, compounded of greed and fear and God knows what else? Men are complicated creatures, some more complicated than others, and our complications eat at us. Our fascination with gangsters stems from the pleasant fantasy that they have razored away the troublesome complexities of life by a sheer, brutal act of will. My fascination with Longy Zwillman began when I first encountered the astonishing fact that a Jew of my grandfather's generation, a man who lived his last years as a thoughtful New Jersey suburbanite, had not only taken up organized crime as a trade but had excelled at it. Tony Soprano became the world's most famous Jersey gangster as the victim, rather than the master, of his complexities. But before Tony came Longy, and Longy was real.

Criminals use aliases, and Abner Zwillman employed several in his working life: he was known variously as George Long, A. Long, Abe Spitzel, and Al Williams. But Longy was the nickname that stuck, and he never liked it. It came from the Yiddish *der Langer*, the tall one, an epithet first bestowed on him on the sidewalks of the Prince Street ghetto of Newark's Third Ward, where, at twelve years old and six feet two—in an era when the average height of an adult American male was five-seven—he acquired a reputation for defending the neighborhood, with his fists, from raiding gangs of pushcart-overturning, *payess*-pulling Irish hoods. Abner was fourteen when his father, a street seller of live chickens, died in the great influenza epidemic of 1918; he dropped out of school after the eighth grade, becoming the sole support of his widowed mother and six brothers and sisters.

At first he took to pushing a cart himself, but since he was as quick with his mind as with his fists, he rapidly found another product that could be sold more profitably door to door than fruits and vegetables—the poor man's hope, the lottery of the day (before the state discovered it could take over and institutionalize what organized crime had, in a sense, only dabbled at): the numbers.

Zwillman soon found that his bosses were dim and shortsighted, given to micro rather than macro thinking. By twenty-one, by force of personality and through coolly planned and strategically applied violence and intimidation, he had graduated from numbers runner to head of the Newark numbers rackets. Inevitably he formed alliances with Lepke Buchalter and Lucky Luciano and Frank Costello across the river in New York, and soon he also established himself as a major bootlegger, in partnership with Sam Bronfman of Montreal and the Reinfeld brothers of Newark. By twenty-six, Longy Zwillman was reputed to be one of the so-called Big Six gangsters in the United States. The other five were said to be Luciano, Buchalter, Benjamin "Bugsy" Siegel, Meyer Lansky, and Jacob "Gurrah" Shapiro—all of New York. In other accounts, Joe Adonis of Brooklyn and Frank Costello replaced Buchalter and Shapiro. In any case, Zwillman was always included. There had been well-known New Jersey criminals before him, but none before Longy had ever taken the reins and gone about the business of organizing crime.

Curiously enough for one in his curious profession, he had the face of a reasonable man—a thick-browed Assyrian face, strong-featured but kindly, even slightly shy when he smiled. The hairline on his broad forehead was low, the heavy dark pelt parted slightly to the left of center. His intelligent, wide-set eyes showed none of the savage opacity or glinting bravado so common in the mug shots and spot-news photos of other men in his line of work. His smile was almost self-effacing. His frown, never photographed, was another matter entirely.

Still, unlike almost every other man in what the era referred to as the rackets, Longy firmly believed in the superiority of tactics to unthinking violence. Violence, in his view, was a tool of last resort. This is not to say that it was a rarely used tool, merely one that he never employed without careful prior consideration. He had evolved somewhat in this regard, from the young hothead in command of his neighborhood to the wise young man of affairs in charge of a small empire.

The defining incident in this shift is telling in itself. In June 1928, a month of record heat in Newark, in an alley behind the Margulies Iron Works on Niagara Street, Zwillman used a tire iron wrapped in a rag to administer a severe beating to one Preston Buzzard, a pimp and numbers runner who had committed what under normal circumstances would be a capital offense: holding back from Zwillman a week's worth of receipts. Rumor had it that Buzzard had used the money to buy a set of false teeth for his mother and a certain amount of liquor for himself, actions that, under his own system of logic, would have felt completely justified. And then, in full outrage at his beating, in defiance of good sense and with no thought of his future, Buzzard—who was a black man— reported the incident to the Newark police.

The Newark police respected Longy Zwillman. By their lights he was a smart, powerful, and useful fellow, a fellow who lived within a certain code—and who, most important, was never stingy when it came to maintaining friendships in the police department. And so the cops collectively cleared their throats and reluctantly went about the business of searching out one of the city's most visible citizens. After the comedy had gone on for a week, Zwillman turned himself in. Once he had been booked and released on $1,000 bail— Zwillman paid cash, the equivalent of over $10,000 today— no fewer than three men came forward to confess that they, not Longy, were guilty of the beating of Preston Buzzard.

None of this made any difference to an ambitious, newly appointed judge named Daniel Brennan, who thought of Zwillman as nothing more than a common street criminal. But miraculously, Brennan's thinking had changed somewhat by the time he sentenced Zwillman to a light term of six months in the Essex County Penitentiary. Zwillman spent his stretch quietly, working as an orderly in the prison hospital and—in a distinctly unorthodox arrangement struck with the warden—leaving on weekends to stay in the house of his bodyguard and driver, Sam "Big Sue" Katz. (Also unlike other inmates, Zwillman had a telephone in his cell, had out-side meals brought in, and enjoyed unlimited visiting privi-leges.) It was the first and last time Abner Zwillman would ever spend behind bars.

Nevertheless, he had learned his lesson. He later said that he had stopped short of killing Buzzard because he felt sorry for him as a black man. It was a genuine, and typical, senti-ment: sympathy for the downtrodden ran deep and intensely in Zwillman. He would give millions to charity over the course of his life, sponsoring scholarships and orphanages and soup kitchens in Newark, buying matzo for indigent Jews on Passover. I would mention the $100,000 reward he offered in the Lindbergh kidnapping were it not for the fact that, if you scrape the surface, you quickly find that federal officers on the lookout for the perpetrator of the Crime of the Century had been stopping Zwillman's liquor trucks in Newark and around the Jersey countryside, gumming up the works of a bootlegging operation so vast that the hundred thousand was a pittance.

Does the surface of his other charitable acts also bear scraping? Even when the subject is gangsters, cynicism can obscure the truth.

Practicality aside, Abner Zwillman was a man of powerful, even elevated, feelings. Like his colleague Lansky—another lonely advocate of brainpower over muscle in the Mob (for the most part)—he had been an exemplary public school student, with good grades and nearly perfect attendance until forced to drop out. He read. He attended the opera. Had he not branched into so many successful criminal enterprises in later life, he might have followed or even trumped his bootlegging partner Reinfeld, who, after the repeal of the Eighteenth Amendment in 1933, would go on to achieve such success as a legitimate liquor importer that he would be created a Knight of the Realm (appropriately Anglicized as Sir Joseph Renfield) by Queen Elizabeth II.

From the beginning, it seemed clear to me, Longy Zwillman wasn't just another gangster. He was a deep man, a man of parts, a prodigious young business mind who, in the instance of Preston Buzzard, simply let his feelings run away with him and neglected a basic principle: an efficient executive delegates responsibility.

● ● ●

By early 1959, though, his Chinese wall was crumbling. Jury tampering was serious business, and the tax evasion case stood to be reopened. Zwillman had comported himself brilliantly before the Kefauver Organized Crime Hearings in 1951—on television!—impressing both the government and his colleagues with his articulate (though highly selective) openness and cool wit. But eight years later there was worry among his colleagues in the upper echelons of organized crime that the investigations might be reopened and that an older and sicker Longy might start to talk.

I have combed every known account of what happened at 50 Beverly Road, West Orange, New Jersey, in the early-morning hours of February 26, 1959. I like to think that my intense interest is more than morbid curiosity—that my need to understand the uncommon end of this uncommon life stems, ultimately, from a wish to know something about myself.

The details surrounding Longy Zwillman's life (we know what clothes he wore, what car he drove, what brand of whiskey he drank) and last days (we know what restaurant he ate in on his last night; we know that he left early, in apparent emotional distress) are remarkably well documented. We know he was taking a medication called reserpine to treat both high blood pressure and agitation. What we don't know is exactly what happened in his final hour.

Yet the part of me that needs to understand him knows deeply.

In the master suite of his West Orange mansion, sometime in the deep watches of the night, he got out of the bed he had lain sleepless in for hours, told his half-awake wife he was going to make himself some warm milk, and shuffled downstairs in his Brooks Brothers slippers and Sulka robe. He went down the back steps but, instead of turning into the kitchen, proceeded along the first-floor hall to his study and took a half-empty bottle of Old Overholt from the bar. He sat in a leather armchair for a long time, looking at nothing, then clutched a handful of pills out of the pocket of his robe and washed them down with a few swallows of whiskey. After a few minutes, the bottle still in hand, he stood unsteadily and walked back up the hall to the cellar door.

The huge finished basement was clean and dry, fragrant with the odors of fresh laundry and leather furniture. There was another full bar down here, a ten-foot slate pool table, a Ping-Pong table, a new RCA color television, a huge wooden console model. Gay travel posters: Rome, Paris, London. A dehumidifier hummed, working steadily against the encroachment of moisture through the stone walls: the big house had been built in a rhododendron-thick glen, alongside a chuckling brown brook. The fluorescent lights, too, hummed. Zwillman took a few more swallows of the Scotch, then stuck the bottle in his robe pocket.

Pleasure and utility had been carefully segregated when the basement was finished: furnace, laundry, and tool rooms were all behind closed doors. Opening the door to the tool room, he at once found what he was looking for, although he was beginning to stagger from the effect of the liquor and the pills. He turned off the light in the tool room, closed the door, and opened another door, this one leading to an unfinished section of basement containing shelves full of clean, ironed, neatly stacked spare sheets and towels. Here the ceiling was just beams. By his calculation, he was directly under the dining room floor. Struggling against sleep but proceeding with great certainty, he stood on a wooden seltzer box, looped the forty-foot black electrical cord he had found over a joist, and tied a double square knot in it. Thick, strong hands, puffy with age and medication. The other end he tied tightly around his neck. Forgive me, Mamele, he said, as he stepped off the soda box.

From the early 1900s to the present time, gangsters have murdered one another with such great efficiency and frequency that law enforcement has rarely seen the need to risk men bringing them in. And suicide is extremely rare, and always suspect. In the wake of Longy Zwillman's death, rumors spread that his body had been discovered with the hands bound—that he had been executed to keep him from talking, the pills and liquor administered to him a token of respect for a man widely revered in his business. From his exile in Sicily, Lucky Luciano backed up the claim.

Yet Luciano was five thousand miles away and long past his days of influence, an old man himself, dreading oblivion and not averse to making pronouncements when there was someone around to take notes. And while it is true that Mob hits can be ordered up from a distance, conspiracy is always a murky subject, and never murkier than in the field of human endeavor misleadingly called organized crime, that night-for-day world where mental deficiency is no handicap and lying more the norm than truth.

Who knows why and how rumors start? Sometimes they are started on purpose; more often, I suspect, a slight misunderstanding—a slip of the eye or ear, rather than of the tongue, what Freud referred to as parapraxis—trips a switch leading from the all-too-fragile line of everyday sensibility to the nighttime realm of the unconscious. There was electrical cord around his neck; he tied the knots with his own hands— or were his own hands tied? Witness the notorious unreliability of eyewitnesses: the eye believes what it wants. In a way, self-destruction is more terrifying than murder, and so there was a vested human interest—even, if not especially, among hardened mobsters—in believing that Longy was hit.

But I'll tell you this: Longy Zwillman died with seven thousand books in his house, and those books weren't just there for wall covering; he had read a good number of them. The Bible, the Talmud, the classics—the Greek tragedians, Shakespeare, Tolstoy and Dostoevsky and Melville and Ralph Waldo Emerson. Herman Wouk and Leo Rosten and Irwin Shaw, of course. And—also of course—the fifteen shelf-feet of published transcript of the Kefauver Hearings on Organized Crime.

All this distinguished Zwillman greatly from almost all his colleagues, even in the upper echelons of crime, where a quick and vicious cleverness is infinitely more valued—if not more valuable—than the thoughtfulness of a broad and reasoned understanding of the world. But dead he was just another dead gangster with a colorful, slightly ribald nickname—a Jewish gangster, it's true, but a dead gangster, nonetheless, one of many. A footnote, a sheaf of fading press clips.

●　　●　　●

My family arrived in the Oranges about forty-five days, by my rough calculation, after Longy Zwillman left the earth. Yet in April 1959, his death would still have been buzzing in the molecules of suburban air: air stirred by the Judeo-Christian strictures against suicide; the raffish glamour of a gangster's presence in, and violent subtraction from, the quiet leafy streets; the shock waves through the social network. Zwillman had relatives in the vicinity; I would come to know, glancingly, a niece and nephew of his when I got to junior high and high school.

What was all this to me? In the spring of 1959, I was naturally if not willfully ignorant of death, violence, crime. I was seven and a half years old, floating dreamily through the leafy haze of a comfortable suburban childhood. My knowledge of personal pain was limited to the following: my father's absences on business trips, my parents' spats, my exclusion from the impenetrably sophisticated social fabric of my new community. We had moved from a farming valley in rural Pennsylvania—my grandfather, seeking ever-cheaper labor for his dwindling men's shirt company, had leased, in nearby Hazleton, a factory that my father managed. From tiny Conyngham, where my crew-cut or pigtailed classmates wore plaid flannel and denim and spoke slowly, to the Oranges, an incomprehensible world of big houses with wide lawns, of wall-to-wall carpeting and Cadillacs, of winter vacations in Florida and maid's night off on Thursdays.

It was, of course, definitively a world of Jews, Jews who had moved up to the suburbs from the hard streets of Newark, Jews who strove ceaselessly to efface the memories and characteristics of a squalid background. Longy was one of them. They attended *shul* on High Holy Days, they davened passionately while they mourned the dead and thanked God that never again would they have to smell the neighbors' cooking and hear their spats in a blue air shaft, never again would they have to walk up four flights of steps and sniff the shit of a communal bathroom.

The women forgot more easily than the men, settled more smoothly into a life of manicures and pedicures, of shopping at Saks and Lord & Taylor, of lounging by the country club pools. The men worked as if their lives depended on it, always looking over one shoulder, afraid it would all fall apart and they would have to go back. Newark lived on in them. Maybe this alone explains Longy's attraction to crime: in understanding what legitimate business really was and what democratic government really was—a struggle for power by the strongest possible means, with the fewest possible chances for getting caught if you happened to step over the line—perhaps he simply wanted to insure his and his family's security, to cover all bases. To hedge his bets.

By way of insurance, he made sure that men in high places owed him favors: he delivered votes to Franklin Roosevelt in 1932 in return for the governor's implicit promise not to turn the Mob-friendly Jimmy Walker out of the mayoralty of New York City. Some years later, he was instrumental in installing a compliant dentist named Meyer Ellenstein as mayor of Newark.

Men loved Longy Zwillman. He had a talent for winning admiration, a gift, even, for turning enemies, both real and potential, into friends by inspiring fear, then doing favors. By having his men put eight bullets into Ruggiero "Richie the

Boot" Boiardo—an assault that Boiardo miraculously survived—he was able to persuade his only real rival in Newark to ally with him. Once it was clear that Boiardo was going to live, Longy extended a friendly hand. And more: in honor of the new alliance, he presented the Boot (so nicknamed because of his penchant for conducting all his business from phone booths) with a diamond-studded belt buckle, a gift of mythic significance that literally saved Richie's life when it stopped a bullet during another murder attempt a few years later. Boiardo wore the buckle until he died in bed at age ninety-five.

But Longy lost in the end through his own humanity, which included a kind of naive belief in the humanity of others, in the power of gratitude to protect him. Roosevelt turned against Walker and the mobs the minute the votes he needed were in his pocket. Ellenstein proved to be of limited use. And despite Longy's agreeing to play ball with the FBI on several key occasions, J. Edgar Hoover felt no obligation at all. Zwillman's tough old friend Meyer Lansky managed to live to a riper (but not much happier) old age by never trusting anybody.

What, in the end, was Longy Zwillman to me? Gangsters compel us because they represent the dark side, acting out on all the instincts the rest of humanity is forced to suppress. Longy was this, but he was something else, too, and the other thing he was made me feel I could begin to understand him.

But I guess what ultimately compelled me about Longy was simply (and not so simply) this: we lived in the same place.

# THE MUSE OF NEW JERSEY

## CATHI HANAUER

EXIT 145

f it's true you can never go home again, it's got to be equally true you can never really leave. At least, not if you're me and the place you're trying to kiss good-bye is New Jersey. I've been gone for almost twenty-five years now, and I certainly can't imagine ever moving back, although every time I visit my parents in West Orange (that's 145 on the parkway) and drive by the old Mitola's, where I spent high school lunch periods snarfing roast beef subs with vinegar, oil, and extra mayo on a mountain of meat atop a football-sized roll, believe me, I'm tempted. And yet, with each year and mile I put between myself and my Jersey childhood—and with all the places I've lived since (London, New York State, New York City, Arizona, Manhattan again, and now western Massachusetts)—lately I find myself admitting, if not actually *offering up*, that I'm a Jersey Girl.

Go figure. Because for years—and I apologize in advance for this confession—I tried desperately to deny, or at least disguise, my suburban New Jersey roots. To me, this took the form of wearing looser clothes (I could zip them without lying down!), lower shoes (who knew girls could actually bend their knees when they walked?), jeans without large designer labels displayed prominently on my butt. I cut my "big" hair into a bob (I looked all wrong, like Debra Winger in *Betrayed*), listened to girl bands from down south, ate thick-crust pizza you couldn't fold down the middle if you tried, and bought a Volvo. (Gag! My high school friends wouldn't dare be seen with me.) And yet, here I am, middle-aged, with a dog named "Rosalita" (yes, after Bruce's Rosalita), my hair long and wild again, and a feeling of dismay when my children, Manhattan-born and Massachusetts-raised, pronounce water as "wah-ter" or coffee "cah-fee." I want to yell, "It's WOR-ter! It's CAW-fee! What are you, from Chi-CAW-go?!"

Both of my novels—written ten years apart—are set in the Jersey suburbs: the first, *My Sister's Bones,* in West Berry, loosely based on West Orange; the new one, *Sweet Ruin,* in an unnamed Jersey commuter hub that's a cross between Maplewood, Montclair, and the New England college town where I live now. It's not that I haven't tried other fictional settings—midtown Manhattan, Tucson's desert—but they just didn't have the character of New Jersey . . . or characters, I should say. There isn't a "type" I've observed from any of these places (no, not even New York) who's as distinctive, lively, and frankly just plain funny as the people I remember from Jersey and the fictional characters they've spawned for me. "Cindi and Joey," for example, from *Sweet Ruin*. She's a sun-worshiping single mother who says things like "I was hysterical crying" and calls everyone by a three- or four-syllable name (Cynthia, Zachariah) even if they don't actually have one; he's a newly Buddhist personal trainer who favors wrestling singlets, bumper stickers, and woven ankle bracelets. Let me tell you, I had more fun writing scenes with Cindi and Joey than just about anything else in that book. In *Bones,* there was the narrator's boyfriend, a wrestler named Vinnie DiNardio, who was as wide as he was tall and said things like "Don't get all hypodermic about it" but was a real peach; and the narrator's best friend, Tiffany Zefferelli, the tough-talking daughter of a New Jersey bookie.

Tiffany was, surprise surprise, inspired by my real-life Jersey childhood best friend, who, along with her family—I'll call them the Pizarros—epitomized, and still does to some extent, New Jersey for me. No matter that they were fresh from Staten Island when we met and would move on, a decade later, to Texas. And no matter that not all of New Jersey was like this (Basking Ridge, the woodsy WASP-ville where my sister lives now, and Princeton, home of, well, *Princeton,* are two places that jump to mind that are not)— and maybe none of it is anymore. West Orange, for one, is now a mecca of diversity, a place where transplanted young white highly educated Brooklyn families—commuting fathers, stay-at-home or part-time working mothers—share blocks and schools with first- and second-generation Haitian, Dominican, Asian, Indian, and Latino families, to name a few. But my New Jersey was and is the Pizarros, and to me, they were the ultimate Jersey girls: four Farrah-haired starlets and their young, zaftig, peroxide-blond mother, a martini-sipping, Winston-smoking, loud-laughing, late-sleeping Sicilian Italian who, when not in a long T-shirt or babydoll nightgown, dressed in spike heels, tight jeans, short white rabbit fur coats, and hot rollers (the jumbo set of which was permanently plugged in at their house). She was everything my own thin, proper, turtleneck-wearing, balanced-meal-providing, PTA-leading, Halloween-costume-sewing, sweetly firm elementary school teacher of a mother was not. My mother, whose idea of a swear word was "Jeepers!" and who simply would not ever, for any reason, utter the words "Bah fongool." Which, of course, only made the Pizarros all the more exciting for me.

My main memory of "Tiffany's" two older sisters—I'll call them Tina and Gina—is them leaning, in tandem, in their amply filled bras and (yup) hot rollers, out the windows of their turretlike second-floor hallway (their house was pink stucco, I kid you not, like a fairy-tale castle with an Italian Jersey touch) to tell me "Tiffy" was still asleep, but I was welcome to come wake her up. (No easy task; first I had to get Tina or Gina to come down and unlock the door, and then— well, let's just say I was in awe of Tiffany's teenlike ability to sleep away the day, when I could rarely sleep past 8:15 A.M., and even when I could, my father, a work-loving physician, woke me up.) Mr. Pizarro, for his part, was a big, overwhelmed teddy bear of a guy who somehow put food on the table, Ludwig drum sets under the Christmas tree, and steering wheels, attached to little white cars, into his daughters' hands—all the better for them to cruise around in while not attending school, Aretha Franklin and Donna Summer blaring from the speakers.

And so what if once in a while their phone service got shut off because they "forgot" to pay the bills? They all still had *fun*—and this is what I took from them, something that's still with me. Mr. P. alternately paced the place wringing his hands at the latest predicament his daughters, dog, or wife had gotten into (the time Tiff and I exploded purple spray paint all over the kitchen, say, or when Benny, their poodle, ate a box of crayons and pooped little rainbows all over the yard) and sat at the table, napkin tucked in his collar, gushing, "Honey! These meatballs, honey! Honey, you've outdone yourself!" (It was true, too. Mrs. P.'s meatballs, the size of Pro Penns, melted like butter as they passed between your lips.) Mrs. Pizarro was many years younger than her husband and as young at heart as her teenage daughters were in actual age. Rumor was that when she and Mr. P. first met, she lied to him about her age by, oh, six years or so, and by the time he found out she was sixteen and not twenty-two to his twenty-eight, give or take, he was already hooked by her enormous blue eyes, girlish laugh, and wish for him to take her away and make a proper woman of her.

And he did. He gave her the ring and then the house in the Jersey suburbs, and she filled it with their girls. And if they weren't quite the sons he'd maybe hoped for, well, boys came along soon enough. When the Pizarro girls weren't sleeping, applying makeup, dieting, breaking their diets, dancing to the latest WBLS disco hit, or doing their hair, they were on the couch watching the soaps with their boyfriends or down in the basement, where there was always a pool game in play. These games featured guys with names like Carlos and Rickie, twenty-something men with hair slicked back and Betty Boop tattoos on their biceps that danced as they aimed their cue sticks, cigarettes glued to their bottom lips. Around the table would be stashes of Mr. or Mrs. P.'s latest hobby or business endeavor: the Shaklee diet powder she sold for a while, various products from the superette he owned down on Main Street for a year or two. (The Pizarro girls all worked the deli and registers and never seemed to actually ever charge anyone—"G'head, take the sandwich, pay next time," they'd say, wagging a hand—until Mr. P. finally sold the place and moved on to other things.)

Once, there were boxes and boxes of shoes Mr. P. had brought home from somewhere: sparkly silver-and-black pumps, skinny-heeled maroon sandals, gold-and-purple "platforms." They were rich! Or, okay, they *would* be, as soon as he got the business off the ground. And for weeks, teenage girls, friends of Tina and Gina, streamed into and out of the house, hair cemented to great heights as they teetered around the basement trying on shoes, telling each other how "absolutely GAW-geous" they looked, how "ohmigod, *so* sharp." In the end, half the shoes disappeared into the Pizarros' own closets or corners of the basement or yard—some chewed to shreds by Benny, others used as hammers by Tiffany and me as we worked on our "clubhouse" (the crawl space under the kitchen), still others simply kicked off during someone's Tab or cigarette break and never retrieved. And then there was the time we all had to hide in the basement, crouched down quiet as mice, while two men in dark suits rang the doorbell again and again, finally giving up and swaggering back to their cars—white El Dorados, black Lincoln Continentals, windows as tinted as the yet-to-be-invented Ray-Bans—and we all stood back up, straightened our skin-tight clothes, and breathed a sigh of relief. I never did know for sure what Mr. P. did when he wasn't at home, but whatever it was, I'd be surprised if he didn't know some of the early Sopranos—the ones who no doubt inspired the decades-later show.

I could write a whole trilogy about the Pizarros, and maybe someday I will. After all, "Tiffany" is the one who pulled me into the New Jersey I would come to know, love, and leave yet never quite truly depart. ("You can take a girl out of Jersey," says one of the characters in *Sweet Ruin,* and you know the rest.) She pulled me away from Ann S.—my quiet, studious first best friend who wanted to become a vet someday and then actually did—and into the world of Tonys and Frankies, of Donnas and Angelas and Marias, of thick necks with thick chains with Italian horns dangling from them, of thick black hair gleaming in headlights as drivers leaned out their car windows to yell, "'Ey! 'Sup! You goin' to Anthony's party tonight, or what?" Tiffany pulled me into the world of tiny tough girls with big shoes and the boys who loved them, of tight huckapoo shirts unbuttoned too low and then pinned strategically at the point to reveal the most boob with the least bra. (So what if the pin showed? We cared not.) And I fit right in, at least on the surface. She and I played a mean game of touch football—with her "quartering" and me at tight end, we were known to crush boys twice our size—

but we knew, too, how to sweet-talk macho Coach Miller (Coach, we have *craaamps!* We *caaan't* do gym class today!"), and we knew when it was time to quit marching band—we both played trumpet—to don tiny red skirts and fluffy pom-poms and cheer on our boyfriends' football team.

With Tiffany, I ventured "down the shore"—Belmar, Toms River, Seaside Heights—and joined the line of West Orange teenagers piling into Evy and Ivan's tiny beach house. Evy and Ivan were our friend Arlene's parents—Arlene was the baby of their collective kids from several marriages—and they welcomed anyone who knew her to stop by and stay for a while. We slept wherever we found a spot, emerging in the morning to troll the boardwalk in bikinis, baby oil, and Candies "Come Fuck Me" shoes for the girls, "guinea Ts" for the guys (hair already blown back Danny Zucco style), stopping first for warm doughnuts from the bakery where Arlene worked and later for cheese steaks and meatball sandwiches on the boardwalk. With Tiffany as my coveted sidekick—she was cool, she was Italian, everyone loved her—I took it all in, so that later, I know now—when she and her family were gone, leaving nothing behind but their house—I could immortalize it all in a book about a shy Jewish girl with a best friend from a warm, wacky Italian family that disappears.


It's the people who make a place, of course, and then, in return, the place comes to form the people. Not that parts of New Jersey aren't like this too, but where I live now is rife with natural beauty: fiery sugar maples in fall, sparkling lakes and rivers in summer, families of black bears, mothers and their cubs, trekking across my front lawn in spring. (Way too much snow in winter, but what can you do?) Except for my town itself—a lively, left-leaning college hub full of lesbians, writers, professors, shrinks, holistic healers, street people, and musicians—western New England seems made mostly of subtle, good country folk, the sort who grow their own fruit for jam and don't throw popcorn in your hair at the movies, the sort among whom it's a pleasure to own a house, raise your children, share a school and a town center with. I like living here at the moment: I like how it tones me down just a bit, I like the people it's making my kids into. But periodically I run into someone from New Jersey—there are more of us up here, I think, than most New Englanders would like to admit—and when I do, there's an instant connection, a banter we immediately seem to fall into. "You're from Jersey too? Get out! *Bloomfield?* No way! Did you know Paulie Castellano? Dominick Perroni? Trez Di Martino? You're kidding me!" I can feel myself let down my guard at those times, feel that age-old Jersey girl part of me surface and stretch, thrilled to be freed from its cage.

Those times, and—go figure again—when I sit down to write. Because what comes out is not the maples and gleaming icicles of New England, not the eerily beautiful Arizona desert with its stately saguaros and armored reptiles that dart among them, and only sometimes the urban jungle of Manhattan, with its intensity of smells, tastes, and sounds, its swarming, scurrying, stunning human mass. But New Jersey, my New Jersey, the New Jersey suburbs . . . well, there it is, on the page. The pizza places and malls, the gas stations and manicured country clubs, featuring tiny tan women and buff, olive-skinned lifeguards killing time between morning and evening workouts; the traffic and highways and toll plazas, change flung from car windows into those wide scratched-up white plastic bins. And the air-conditioned homes in which people like the Pizarros laugh and cook "macaronis" and "pasta fazool" and shoot pool and try on shoes and curl their eyelashes and drink Amaretto and "martoonis." It's a setting I love to relive, a setting that speaks to and inspires me. Why else would I write about it again and again? It's my way of staying close, of never really leaving. No matter how long I've been gone or how far gone I am.

EXIT 15W

JOSHUA BRAFF

EXIT 15W

"**N**ew York" is how my friend from New Jersey has always chosen to answer the question "Where are you from?" In fact he says it twice, "New York, New York," and does so with a certain swagger, a certain "Made it here, can make it anywhere" vibe that's pitiful, really, especially because it's assumed I won't call him out on his fib or tell the inquirer that he's actually from Nutley and now lives in Hoboken. He doesn't lie about his age or his height or the fact that he shaved his oddly shaped head for fashion's sake and not necessity. Recently, after he said it again, "New York, New York," I started thinking that he may just feel his apartment is close enough to Manhattan to warrant the answer. In truth, barring PATH train congestion, he can be in *his* city with a *Village Voice* under his arm in less than twenty minutes. And now that I think about it, his passion for Woody Allen and Bernadette Peters and Tino Martinez and Papaya Juice is far superior to any Lakeridge or Parsippany or Cherry Hill resident's I've ever met. Perhaps my "New Yorker" friend is simply trying to avoid being asked if he's "from Joyzy?" or "Which exit?" he lives off, or if he loves *"Bruuuuce!"* He does work in the city and socializes in the city and wears a lot of black. I say if he feels in his heart of hearts that he's better defined on that side of the river, then who is it hurting, really?


I've never had any trouble being proud of the fact that I'm from New Jersey. I was born in Perth Amboy, lived in Matawan for eleven years, and moved to South Orange in 1978. My father used to tell me that New Jersey was unique because there was no hiding from the seasons. He saw a certain honesty in the way autumn gently prepared us for winter and how the spring brought light breezes before the roast of summer settled in. "And the beaches," he continued, "and the mountains and the diversity and the people and what about the Jersey Girls?" "What about them?" I asked, and he thought for a moment and started to sing: "Nothin' else matters in this whole wide world, when you're in love with a Jersey Girl. Sing sha la la, la la la." I found this to be a pretty vague explanation, and his wife, my mother, was from Providence, so that made no sense. But a few years later, in the seventh grade, I kissed my first Jersey Girl at the top of Redmond Road, about a block from her house. She had smooth olive skin, green eyes, and long brown hair that coiled in loose curls to the middle of her back. It was a quick kiss. On the lips. A little disappointing, considering Susan Dozer had put her tongue in my mouth at her Bat Mitzvah party just one week earlier at the West Orange Manor. But after the peck I watched the Jersey Girl walk across Wyoming Avenue and onto her front porch. And it's there, right there, I felt it. An undeniable wave of euphoria; an actual first jolt of love. For me this meant that tongue or no tongue, nothing was going to stop me from calling this Jersey Girl my own. Except Denise Greenfield. Denise mashed her closed lips against mine during a late-night bus ride home from Action Park. Unlike the peck, this form of kissing lasted longer and I couldn't wait to walk up Redmond Road and introduce it to my Jersey Girl.

Unfortunately, Larry Fine was on that bus too and had Spanish with Leslie Newport, who had second-period gymnastics with the Jersey Girl, who was approached by Leslie and told the bad news. My love found me at my locker, just outside Ms. Kerrigan's science lab, and said she'd "need to break up with me." I walked slowly up Scotland Road that day and to my house on Charlton. I knew I'd made an enormous mistake. I'd tasted the fruit that was Denise Greenfield. And my lust had cost me.

· · ·

In the years to come, I'd see my Jersey Girl between classes in the halls of Columbia High with her arm around a lacrosse player the cheerleaders called Smitty. Smitty was muscular and athletic and so handsome that his acne came off as endearing. He was rumored to have consumed a pony keg of Piels at a legendary party while his best friend's parents visited Mount Airy Lodge. He got his stomach pumped at Saint Barnabas that night and missed a crucial playoff game with Millburn that would cost Columbia the crown that year. But Smitty didn't care. He had my Jersey Girl in the passenger seat of his Camaro, even draped his lacrosse jacket over her shoulders as she clutched his oak tree arms. Nothing could be sweeter for old Smitty and my girl. She was smart and funny and easy to be around, with a smile that lit her eyes up like little green jewels. He was a homophobe with a size fifteen shoe and two DUIs. And as they walked arm in arm into the cafeteria each day, turning every head in the room, I knew, just as everyone did, that my Jersey Girl would never let him go.

The autumn air of 1984 turned to ice quite quickly, and a rumor hit the halls of Columbia High and spread like wildfire: Captain Smitty had "gone sledding" in the reservation with superslutty Marnie Bukowski, thus bringing a thrilling and sudden halt to the relationship of the century. My Jersey Girl walked into the cafeteria alone. She was wounded, I could see it in her eyes, embarrassed by the image of Marnie's hand down old Smitty's sweatpants. The mean girls snickered, and the jocks kept quiet. I felt for her and thought about approaching her. But I didn't. I couldn't. And when the brutal winter gave way to yet another glorious New Jersey spring, the humid days of summer soon followed and everyone I knew headed to Long Beach Island. There I would see her, my Jersey Girl, at a house party in Loveladies, sipping Stroh's on the lap of a wrestler the cheerleaders called Fitsy. Bon Jovi's "Livin' on a Prayer" cranked from the stereo as beer-chubby, sunburned girls in boxer shorts shimmied on tables where the drinking games "quarters" and "chandeliers" were inebriating the entire upper class. One girl named Willa Krane, whose hot pink boxers said "Bull's Eye" across the ass, asked me if I wanted to take a walk with her on the beach. As I yelled "okay" over the music and stood to leave, I noticed my Jersey Girl glancing over at me while Fitsy placed a pinch of Skoal between his cheek and gum. My Jersey Girl was watching me. My Jersey Girl seemed to care that I was leaving. She didn't want me to go down to the beach with Willa "Bull's Eye" Krane, not one bit. I stopped on the porch with Willa's hand in mine and sat her down. And when I looked into her barely focused, bloodshot eyes to tell her there was someone else in my life, she burped twice before vomiting on the hedges. "That's right," I said to myself, returning to the party. There's only one girl for me. And there she is now, sitting on Fitsy's lap, laughing at something he said, kissing his chin, his ear, his cheek, his tobacco-stained lips. Willa didn't look so good when I went back to find her. I asked her if she thought she'd be sick again, and she scrunched her nose up and said, "Yes." We made our way back to the hedges, and I asked if she still wanted to take that walk on the beach. She glanced at me with squinty eyes and scrunched her nose up the same way. I took it as a no.

Prom time. A rented tux from the Livingston Mall. Shiny red bow tie with matching cummerbund. Mirror-shined patent-leather shoes, a refrigerated carnation, and yes, a freshly groomed mullet. The mullet was not yet considered a felony of fashion in 1986. Bono had one, Andre Agassi, all the members of Def Leppard, and my date, Heather Frye, an Ozzy fanatic I had met at the Brendan Byrne Arena during the "Blizzard of Oz" tour. Together we raised our devil-horn fingers toward the ceiling of the Meadowlands and pumped our fists to the speed of "Crazy Train." Heather was the girl for me. With her big Aqua Netted hair and white leather jacket bought from the Union Market, there was no real reason to think about my Jersey Girl anymore. I hardly even noticed that her prom date was a baseball player the cheerleaders called Wellsy. Legend held that Wellsy once hit a ball at Underhill field that traveled 400 feet before rolling another mile and a half toward Chatham. He was muscular and handsome and all that crap, but with Heather Frye on my arm, none of it mattered anymore. And when she excused herself once again to blow lines off the toilet seat at the Bayonne Hilton, I watched Wellsy spin and dip his date as she sang along to the gentle words of Springsteen's "Tunnel of Love." And that's when I knew. Right then. I'd been fooling myself. I still loved my Jersey Girl. I did. But the peck I'd received on Redmond Road was as far as we were ever going to go. I took my mullet and my coke-fiend date home that night and by morning had rid myself of both.

I heard my Jersey Girl went to Colgate after high school, and then a friend of mine mentioned that she'd transferred out west. I graduated from NYU in '91 and got a job teaching English as a second language at a school in Tokyo. A week before I left for Japan, my "New Yorker" friend and I were in a bar in Hoboken called Scotland Yard. The Yard, as it was known, had live blues on Monday nights, and a guitar player named Willy Sands had just left the stage. Nirvana's "Smells like Teen Spirit" played repeatedly from the jukebox in the corner as my "New Yorker" friend did his third shot of tequila. He was heartsick that day because his girlfriend slept with her sister's husband's brother's buddy while camping in Mount Vernon. "The guy's from Michigan," he kept saying, "but he told her he lived in France. He doesn't live in France, his mother does." He stroked his still bald head with both his hands and clenched his jaw to avoid tears. "I loved her, man," he said softly. "I loved her."

And that's when it happened. There was a soft tap on my shoulder and a "Hey there" from a gentle voice I remembered well. When I turned, my Jersey Girl stood before me. Her dark hair was longer but straight now, her face still stunning, more defined, mature. And those amazing green eyes. They were exactly the way I remembered them. Only now they were focused on me for the first time since that peck on

Redmond Road. I introduced her to my "New Yorker" friend, who waved without looking up, and I grabbed her a chair. I asked her where she lived now, and she said, "Jersey, here, Hoboken, a few blocks from the PATH." She told me she'd moved only a week before and now worked for an ad agency in Manhattan. My "New Yorker" friend lifted his head and asked her what street she lived on. She said Fifth and Garden, and he nodded and found a smile. She asked him where he lived, and he looked at me and blinked a few times before answering. "Born and raised in Jersey," he finally said. "I live at Eighth and Willow." I'd never heard him give his actual address before. Maybe it was her. Maybe there was something about my Jersey Girl that made pretending you're someone you're not useless. Maybe this is what my father meant all those years ago, when he spoke of the seasons and the uniqueness of New Jersey and the people born here. "We're practically neighbors," my "New Yorker" friend said with a smirk and pulled his chair closer to hers. And the rest goes a little bit like this. My Jersey Girl and I leave "The Yard." That night we kiss on the front stoop of her Hoboken apartment (yes, tongue). Wednesday we eat the famously delicious and thin crusted pizza of Bunnie's Saloon on South Orange Avenue and get two Dusty Roads to go from Grunning's. Thursday we talk about the fact that we like each other quite a bit but that I have a job teaching English in Asia that starts on Monday. Friday morning, next to her in bed, I watch her sleep and have a very strong feeling that I still love my Jersey Girl and how this is terrible timing considering I have a job teaching English in Asia that starts on Monday. Six months later I surprise her by coming home three weeks early. Two years later we get married. Five years later we have a baby boy. Three years later we have a baby girl.

My Jersey Girl and I don't live in Jersey anymore. We live where the seasons are less distinct and where no one can make pizza or bagels like they do back home. But when people ask us where we met, I never hesitate to answer. "New Jersey," I say. "Exit 15W."

# HORIZON HOUSE

## FREDERICK REIKEN

EXIT 18W

When I was in fifth grade, the teenage son of a local mobster ran me over with his bicycle. I was in Fort Lee, staying with my father for the weekend at a high-rise complex called Horizon House. It was April 1977, and I was playing tennis with a boy named Ian Friedman, who lived with his mother and his sister at Horizon House. I was just about to serve when the mobster's son and another kid rode their bikes onto the complex's private tennis courts. Then the mobster's son announced that he was going to run me over.

At the time, I didn't know he was a mobster's son. What I

knew was that there was no reason for this boy or his much larger friend to run me over. I knew this because I was from Livingston, where upper-middle-class Jews and Italians lived on the same block and where you could play tennis on public courts without worrying that anyone would run you over. So I stood there, assuming he was bluffing. He rode right at me and didn't stop. Next thing I knew, I was on my back. To a certain extent, I think the mobster's son was just as surprised as I was. He must have assumed that I would jump out of the way. Miraculously unhurt, I grabbed my racket and was about to run for my life when the kid picked up his bike, climbed onto it, and rode off. His silent acolyte followed after him, and Ian Friedman told me the kid's name and who he was. I didn't play tennis again during the weekends when I visited my father.

This was a time of particular confusion in my life. My parents had separated just after the New Year, and for a few months my father had shared an apartment with one of his recently divorced law partners in Nutley. There was a pool table there, and he had tacked a poster of Farrah Fawcett-Majors to his wall. Strangely enough, my parents continued seeing each other. Stranger yet, they soon began to "date," and sometimes, instead of my sister and me going out to Nutley for the weekend, he would come and stay in Livingston. It looked as if my parents might be getting back together. But then my father moved into a three-bedroom, eighth-floor apartment in Fort Lee.

Before Horizon House, I had been once to a high-rise in the adjacent town of Cliffside Park. There were no high-rises in Livingston. The tallest building was probably three stories, so for me a high-rise in Cliffside Park was a thing that bordered on the exotic. We'd gone there on the day of the Bicentennial to watch Operation Sail, a parade of tall ships from around the world, as they sailed down the Hudson River. The apartment belonged to Ian Friedman's father, whom we called Friedy, and he lived there with his second wife. Friedy and my father had grown up together in Jersey City. Friedy was famous in our family for an incident in which one of our dachshunds ate his socks and, a day later, vomited them back up while greeting Friedy at the door. Friedy was a funny, extremely witty, very likable man, who spoke fast and smoked a lot of cigarettes. He was a bit taller than my father, and he still spoke with the Jersey City accent that my father had worked hard to get rid of (although, when Friedy was around, the accent would return). They were both lawyers and had clerked together for a year after attending different law schools. Since high school, they had been the best of friends.

In certain ways, I blamed Friedy for the fact that, less than a year after the tall ships came down the Hudson, my father moved to Horizon House. His apartment was much like Friedy's. It was a luxury kind of place, with wood floors and high ceilings, so that being on the eighth floor was more like being on the sixteenth. It had a balcony with deck chairs and one chaise longue and a view of the Hudson River. There was a grassy area below and then a line of trees and then, I believe, a steep drop down to the town of Edgewater, which sat level with the river.

While I don't have a strong visual memory of the town of Fort Lee itself, I remember that we could see the Horizon

House apartment complex from far away as we approached on Route 80. We would come through the Meadowlands. We'd smell the methane and other putrid chemicals wafting out over the marshes. We'd pass the exits for towns like Teaneck, Englewood, and Leonia, and on the ridge above would be several clusters of high-rise buildings. We could tell which cluster was Horizon House, and I was able to pick out my dad's building. Then Route 80 would weave up a steep hill, and we would exit just before the entrance to the George Washington Bridge. At that point, the pseudoskyline that was formed by the Fort Lee apartment complexes would be replaced by the skyline of New York.

Incidentally, I am not making up the name Horizon House. Nor is Page Place, the name of the street I grew up on in Livingston, fictitious. And so, in all their cloying metaphor, the pages of Page Place and the horizons of Horizon House came to exist in opposition to each other. Page Place was who I was and Horizon House was a rough and dirty secret I did not talk about with anyone. In Livingston, there were cul-de-sacs and driveways where we played street hockey. There were fenced-in backyards where we played Wiffle Ball. I had a mustard yellow three-speed bike with a banana seat, and on most afternoons I would ride the five blocks from Page Place to Glendale Avenue, where several of my friends lived, and where street hockey games took place almost daily. Other days I rode into Livingston Center to buy comic books and baseball cards from a candy store called Silverman's. Tuesday and Thursday afternoons I was supposed to go to Hebrew school, but my mother was a professed atheist and frequently let me skip it.

Central to all my neighborhood peregrinations was "the brook," a little stream that ran through my suburban development, which before 1969 had been horse pastures and riding trails and dairy farms. There were no trees along the streets, but there was still a swath of trees around the brook, where my friends Brant Cherny, Scott Sherman, and I skimmed stones and seemed to make a big deal of building rock bridges or finding other ways to cross over the four inches of water. We sometimes ran into tough kids who were there doing things like smoking or lighting firecrackers under the cover of the foliage. Occasionally, we had to run for it, but none of these tough kids was the son of a mobster. None of them ever even really threatened us. We just thought it made sense—almost like part of a game—to run.

In a short time, I grew to hate Horizon House. Not only did it symbolize my parents' separation; not only did it seem ugly and desolate, one big parking lot, compared to the quiet, winding streets of Livingston, where I'd lived since I was three; not only did I hate waking very early on Monday mornings so my father could drive my sister and me to our Livingston elementary school before going to his law office in West Orange; I hated that I didn't know who I was there. I had no friends there, other than Ian Friedman, who was more of an acquaintance; more of a default friend, whom I would play with when our fathers got together. Ian didn't seem to mind living at Horizon House. It was his actual life, whereas my visits to Horizon House felt virtual, and the second I returned to my life in Livingston, I would block out the fact that I had ever been there. I would block out the feeling that I had seen something much bigger than whatever I was comfortable with. I would try to forget the random things that didn't really seem like they should happen.

For instance, once, when I was walking across the parking lot, someone threw an apple off of a high balcony. It smashed on the pavement less than fifteen feet away from me. Another time, I accidentally walked right past someone who was snorting cocaine in his car. The man spasmodically got out from the car and warned me that next time I should use the sidewalk and not cut directly across the lot. His tone was menacing and entirely without irony. While I was used to people yelling at me halfheartedly for cutting through backyards in Livingston, this situation did not compute. Was I in danger? Might this man shoot me? Was the mobster's son nearby? Part of me *felt* safe despite all of this, yet there was always something lurking, something much worse than the mobster's son who had run over me with his bicycle, something that threatened or had already dismantled the little box that I imagined to be my world.

Shortly after the incident with the mobster's son, my parents began spending almost every weekend together. Sometimes we'd meet at restaurants. More often, my mother would drive us to Horizon House. Usually I would sit around reading comic books, or I'd play Beatles songs and, endlessly, the theme song from the *Peanuts* television specials on my father's newly acquired baby grand piano. Sometimes I skated around on the hardwood floors in my socks, and I would spend a lot of time out on the balcony, staring out at what, quite literally, seemed the wideness of the world. There was one afternoon when I sat out in the sun and read a novel called *The Winged Colt of Casa Mia*. Another afternoon, we all watched in amazement as a small plane flew under the George Washington Bridge. The balcony wasn't large, and there were balconies above us and below us. There was a black metal guardrail, and I'd lean over it, sometimes precariously, and stare down at the ground.

My parents' fighting—loud arguments that had characterized the year leading up to the separation—resumed sometime that spring, and though there didn't seem to be any particular point of focus, it kept happening, and more than once my mother stormed out and returned to Livingston without us. On one occasion we went with her, and the entire ride she ranted about something. I've forgotten what. I just remember I was glad to be going back to Livingston a day early. Soon the fighting got even worse, and at a certain point my mother announced that there would be no reconciliation. Then she stopped going to Horizon House. Soon after that my parents more or less ceased talking.

One afternoon, when my father was asleep and, for whatever reason, my sister was in Livingston with my mother, I climbed over the railing of the balcony. I held on with one arm and one leg, leaned out, and stared at the grass below me. I barely knew what I was doing. I had just wanted to see what it would feel like. I kept wondering what it might feel like to jump. I didn't jump and did not plan to, but after that strangely hypnotic act, I began to worry that I *might* jump. I began thinking, melodramatically, *I am doomed.* I did it three or four more times. Once was at night, and I recall staring at the lights of New York City. I screwed my eyes up and pretended I was so dizzy I might fall. And always, I imagined what my parents would do if they saw me holding on by one arm and one leg from the balcony. They would recognize that everything to do with the Horizon House was not normal. They would instantly decide that it was time to leave Horizon House, move back in together in Livingston, and restore our former life.

But it was normal. I'd learn that soon enough. It was normal to look out across a river and see the movement of cars along the Henry Hudson Parkway. It was normal, particularly in New Jersey, to be living with ambiguity and a sense of fragmentation. It was normal to feel, simultaneously, the distance and proximity of New York. It was normal to feel both safe and unsafe, to believe in the comfort of our cedar-shingled house on .3 acres on Page Place and also wonder what it would feel like to jump off of an eighth-story balcony. It was normal, all of a sudden, to worry that a mobster's son could show up anywhere on his bicycle, that even though I knew he wouldn't, he'd run me over.

I encountered the mobster's son one other time. I was buying comic books at the Horizon House candy store. When I walked out, he was outside smoking a cigarette and talking to a very attractive girl. This was in June. It was warm and humid. The girl was wearing a yellow one-piece bathing suit and a satiny shiny jacket, zipper unzipped. She had dark hair and puffy lips and catlike eyes. She looked at me as I walked by with my comic book. She flashed a smile, so I smiled and continued walking. I glanced back once and by then she'd looked away. The mobster's son still had not looked at me, or so I thought, so I chanced glancing back a second time. In a matter-of-fact tone, he said, "Start running." I wasn't sure if he meant me. I kept on walking, and then he said, "I told you to *start running.*" I heard the pretty girl laugh, and then I ran.

It wasn't until years later that I told my father about the mobster's son, although I'd asked him many times that year if he thought he'd ever move out of Horizon House. He'd often counter with the "great things" about living there. There was the pool, which we'd been to once with Ian Friedman and his sister, Jemma. There was the view from the balcony, and, of course, there was his baby grand piano. There was Fort Lee's Fulton Fish Market restaurant. There were the trips into New York, to the once-not-so-touristy Serendipity, where we drank sweet frozen drinks and ate hamburgers with bleu cheese. He had a point—there were things I liked. Now, in my memory, I feel pangs of nostalgia for the place. Much as I hated Fort Lee, I also loved it. Or, at least, my memory is almost eidetic when it comes to that Horizon House apartment. I'll sometimes think about certain objects. For instance, the jade lady, an intricately carved and valuable statuette that sat on one of his tall speakers. He'd had a client who couldn't pay his bill, and the jade lady, for that year, served as collateral. I've often seen that skinny, light green, parasol-holding lady in my dreams. He had a telescope there, too. I recall looking at the moon, seeing the "moonsea" that my field guide to astronomy identified as Oceanus Procellarum. Of course, I looked at the skyline of New York and came to know all of the buildings. I'd also look at the people down in Edgewater. Most often, I'd use the telescope to stare at the cars moving along the Henry Hudson Parkway. I'd watch the flow of the cars or note the traffic and announce it to my father. It would delight me not to be stuck in that traffic across the river.

Finally, my dad did move out of Horizon House. It was a few months after Friedy temporarily moved in with him, taking my bedroom while I was away at a summer camp in Maine. Friedy had recently been hospitalized for manic depression. This had followed a violent argument with his wife, and when Friedy was discharged, his wife didn't think he was ready to come home. So she asked my father if Friedy could stay with him for two weeks while he calmed down. He was on lithium and, according to my father, still in a very agitated state. Each morning, he left Friedy sitting on the balcony, where he sat chain-smoking and staring out at the Hudson River. My father called each day to check on him. At night, he would return home and take Friedy out to dinner. This was the pattern for five days, until an evening when my father returned to find the lobby of his apartment building filled with cops. When he entered his apartment, eight or ten plainclothes officers were there waiting. They had been checking every apartment that had a balcony in line with the spot where they'd discovered Friedy's body. My father's was the only one that had not checked out.

Friedy's suicide leap occurred in early July, almost exactly one year after Operation Sail. I didn't hear about it until after I'd returned from summer camp. The most confusing aspect of the tragedy was that it seemed to have brought my parents back together. They'd resumed speaking to one another at Friedy's funeral. They were discussing my father's plans to return to Livingston. The whole thing was unsettling and made no sense to me, but after a day or two the shock wore off, and, strangely, I kept wondering how he had done it. Had Friedy balanced on the top rail and then sprung off? Had he held on by one arm and one leg, the way I had, but then let go? At some point, just before my father vacated the apartment, I climbed out over the rail again. With the circuitous logic of an eleven-year-old, I decided that I was almost-but-not-quite jumping.

My parents' reconciliation did not last long, but for the six or seven months that my father returned to Livingston, I told myself that everything was okay. Our dachshunds slept under the baby grand piano. The jade lady had been returned to the client. Meanwhile, the telescope wound up in our TV room. It seemed odd that there was no longer a river to look over. Still I looked through it sometimes. I'd look at trees or the dogs running around the yard. Sometimes I'd take it into the living room, and from there I could look out onto Page Place. I'd watch the cars come up the hill. I'd watch kids walking by on the sidewalk. I suppose I was just trying to see what was coming toward me. I was trying to see whether it was dangerous. Trying to figure out whether I was safe.

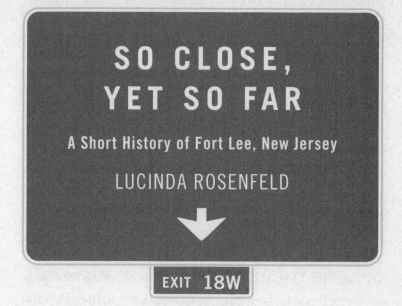

# SO CLOSE, YET SO FAR

A Short History of Fort Lee, New Jersey

LUCINDA ROSENFELD

EXIT 18W

As a young woman, living in New York, I used to be embarrassed about being from New Jersey. It didn't fit in with my fantasy of myself—as a tragic-poet type with impeccable style. If someone asked me where I was from, I'd say, "Just outside the city." (I'd swallow the "in New Jersey" part.) If people asked for specifics, I'd tell them, "Near Englewood." No one had ever heard of my hometown, Leonia. Plus, the name doesn't exactly roll off the tongue. So I usually left that part out, even though, in fact, Leonia, with its shady streets and turn-of-the-century houses, was and is a perfectly nice place to grow up in. I also tried to avoid mention of Leonia's other neighbor up the hill, Fort Lee. The perpetually congested almost-metropolis, with its ubiquitous high-rises overlooking the Hudson, epitomized for me everything that was artless, tacky, and dismal about the region in which I'd been reared.

Growing up, my main association with Fort Lee was the Fort Lee Racquet Club, an indoor tennis bubble in which I spent hundreds of hours of my teenage life practicing my two-handed backhand. As crazy as I was about tennis, I remember being equally enthralled by the cast of characters who populated the place. In the 1980s, Fort Lee's two dominant populations were Jewish and Japanese. (Fort Lee's nickname around Bergen County was "Foto Lee," while politically incorrect jokes abounded about Fort Lee being filled with nothing but "JAPS.") Housewives of both ethnicities kept company in the club's lounge, waiting to pick up their kids and chatting among themselves. Since I couldn't understand Japanese, I listened in on the first group's conversations. In my memories, all the women sport brassy voices and speak endlessly of breast augmentations, time-shares in Aruba, and weight loss plans. When not speaking, they sip Diet Cokes and nibble on bagels and cream cheese, their pinkies and fourth fingers akimbo, revealing tan fingers, long red nails, and numerous jeweled rings. Everyone is named Linda or Marcie and wearing leather pants.

I knew the pros personally. *Brad* was the heartthrob of the lot. A fair-haired, late-twenty-something with a shapely backside he kept on full display in skin-tight, lemon yellow shorts, he was always sliding his hands across the backs of the tennis ladies and, on occasion, their offspring. (A tall, giggling blonde, P.—the daughter of my father's musical instrument dealer—was a special favorite.) A late bloomer, I had no hope of winning that kind of attention from Brad. But I was thrilled by proxy when he took my mother aside after "clinic" and told her, in his mellifluous voice, "Lucinda has the most beautiful strokes."

*Larry*, who was lanky and lightly bearded, was crabbier than Barry but amusing in his own way. He'd yell, "Home run!" if I hit the ball past the baseline. He lived in his car. But you got the feeling that if and when he was offered alternate sleeping accommodations, he didn't decline. In fact, it wasn't hard to imagine that Brad and Larry had been hired as much for their volleying techniques as for their ability to capture the imagination of the students, who, in turn (myself included), kept coming back for more.

My older sisters' Fort Lee, on the other hand, centered around an aging ballet instructor named Mrs. Vogel, who held dance classes in the basement of her modest brick home near Linwood Plaza. Mrs. Vogel's black bun was affixed with mesh wire. To the great fascination of her students, including my sisters, she had taught her pet Chihuahua to do arabesques.

I was in high school, in neighboring Englewood, when the 1985 movie *Desperately Seeking Susan* was released. In the film, Rosanna Arquette plays Roberta, a bored housewife, who is married to a hot tub salesman and lives in a Fort Lee high-rise. Roberta soon becomes obsessed with a wild girl named Susan (played by Madonna), who inhabits the demi-monde of downtown Manhattan. One night, Roberta disappears into the city to follow her doppelgänger around. The two women wind up at a thrift store, where Roberta purchases Susan's old clothes (Susan has discarded them for a new outfit). Dressed as Susan, Roberta is mistaken for the "other woman" by a petty mafioso who has old business to settle with Susan. A blow to the head causes Roberta to lose her memory and imagine, briefly, that she is Susan. For one long night, until she is woken from her dream, Roberta inhabits the other woman's far more exciting life.

I remember loving the movie. (Admittedly, at that point in my life, I was willing to embrace anything with Madonna in it.) But I also remember feeling slightly discomfited on Fort Lee's behalf and, by association, my own. Despite having grown up in Leonia, in a handsome Arts and Crafts house from 1905, overidentified with the nighttime shots of Roberta gazing longingly out the window of her high-rise apartment, at the twinkling lights across the river. Growing up in northern New Jersey, as I did, New York seemed both incredibly close and impossibly far away, bordering on impenetrable. I remember long Saturdays spent wandering through Greenwich Village with my sister, staring at the people on the street and the clothes in the stores and doubting that I would ever be any more than a spectator of life's most electrifying experiences. Like Roberta, I, too, longed to reinvent myself across the river and didn't know how.

Years later—years after I moved to the city and became, I suppose, a passable imitation of one of the people at whom I had once stared—it strikes me as no coincidence that Roberta's character hails from Fort Lee. Upon close inspection, the town is itself a study in reinvention. Maybe that's why, over the last several years, I've developed a strange attachment to the place. Just like the rest of us—but maybe even more so—Fort Lee seems to make a habit of erasing its past.

The fact that Fort Lee became an architectural wasteland is not entirely the fault of Fort Lee's civilians. Vast swaths of undeveloped land were leveled in connection with the building of the George Washington Bridge, which Fort Lee abuts, in the 1920s. (The bridge was completed in 1931.) To deal with the glut of traffic that inevitably followed, highways had to be built and more houses knocked down. But even before the GW's steel beams were being stretched across the Hudson, Fort Lee was attracting trouble.

The fort for which Fort Lee was named dates back to 1776, the first year of the Revolutionary War and also the worst for the independence movement. With the British intent on controlling the Hudson Valley, the American Army, under General George Washington and his second in command, Charles E. Lee (Fort Lee's namesake), went on the defensive. Fort Washington, in upper Manhattan, was erected first. A second fortification—today, the site of Fort Lee Historical Park—went up on the opposite shore. It proved a dismal failure.

After Fort Washington fell to the British—and thousands of American soldiers escaped in row boats across the Hudson—Washington ordered the immediate abandonment of the encampment at Fort Lee (then called Fort Constitution) as well. Short on time, the army fled down (modern-day) Fort Lee Road, abandoning most of their provisions. Things went from bad to worse when the two armies met up at the Battle of Hackensack and the American Army was resoundingly crushed. It was during this same winter that Thomas Paine—

among the soldiers who had fled Fort Constitution/Fort Lee—wrote the famous line "These are the times that try men's souls."

Things were relatively quiet in Fort Lee in the nineteenth century. But with the beginning of the twentieth—and Fort Lee's incorporation in 1904—mayhem returned. A New Jersey resident, Thomas Edison, though most famous for inventing the lightbulb, was also the mastermind behind the Kinetoscope, among the world's first moving-picture cameras. The debate remains as to whether Edison invented motion pictures or not. However, he was undoubtedly the first movie studio titan, and it was in Fort Lee that he set up shop. With its proximity to New York City, combined with its (at that point) still rugged terrain, the town soon attracted other aspiring filmmakers as well. Westerns had become wildly popular during the period, and the Coytesville section of Fort Lee just happened to boast dirt roads and a Wild West–style saloon called Rambo's. Literally overnight, Fort Lee was transformed from a backwater to the center of silent film production in America. The town's residents lined up to play extras. At the height of the era, there were eight American production companies and three French ones operating out of Fort Lee. The term "cliffhanger" actually owes its origin to the many thrill shots taken of actors battling it out on the rocky cliffs of the town. First appearing in *Rescued from an Eagle's Nest,* the Palisades, as the cliffs are known, most famously feature in the classic "women-in-jeopardy" film series *The Perils of Pauline.*

Tired of battling New Jersey winters and paying fees to the monopoly power exerted by the Edison Trust, the film industry eventually headed out to Hollywood. But Fort Lee's "party vibe" prevailed into and beyond the Great Depression. In 1929, a nightclub called Villa Richard, opened by the former chef of Delmonico's, was raided by the police on suspicion of it being a bordello. The sprawling complex eventually became the infamous Riviera nightclub, best known for its illicit gambling activities. After a fire destroyed the property, the Riviera was rebuilt farther south on the Palisades, where it boasted a retractable domed roof and a glitzy neon sign. Its last stage show, in 1953, featured Eddie Fisher and Henny Youngman. (Shortly after closing, the club was knocked down to make way for the Palisades Interstate Parkway.)

From early to midcentury, Fort Lee was also the famed home of the Coney Island–like Palisades Amusement Park, which boasted two hundred rides, including the world's biggest Ferris wheel. (My mother remembers going there on a date with a boy from her high school and throwing up after taking one of the rides.) The park was flattened in 1971 to make way for a high-rise.

The two towers and four midsize buildings that make up Horizon House, completed in the mid- to late 1960s, mark the beginning of Fort Lee's high-rise era. (During high school, my friend N., who lived there with her much older shoe salesman father, would invite me over to "lay out" at HH's outdoor pool, where she slathered baby oil all over her body and baked.) Horizon House was soon followed by the Colony, the Plaza, the Century Towers, Mediterranean Towers (which has its own dentist) . . . the list goes on and on. With their uninspired box construction, Fort Lee's towers are no more or less egregious than anything built across the

Hudson, especially on the East Side, during the same period. It is their context that makes them off-putting. Unencumbered by zoning regulations, many were plopped down in the middle of neighborhoods of one- and two-story buildings and even freestanding homes. As of this essay's writing, there are forty-five high-rises in Fort Lee—more than in any other town or city in New Jersey—and untold numbers still in the process of going up.

Yet Fort Lee's reinvention wheel has hardly slowed down. Recent visits to the neighborhood suggest that, in the last ten years, Fort Lee has transformed itself yet again—this time, into a mini-Seoul (Korean) on the Hudson. Once lined with clothes shops featuring gold lamé evening gowns and paint-splattered sweatshirts, Main Street is now rife with Korean business interests whose signs are unintelligible to this writer. (In recent years, Korean immigrants have become majority or near-majority populations in Palisades Park and Leonia, too.)

Like Fort Lee, I, too, keep evolving. For instance, I'm no longer embarrassed about being from New Jersey. My last novel took place almost entirely in the Garden State. And somewhere along the way, I came to realize that the very definition of a "romantic poet type with impeccable style" is someone from New Jersey who's trying really hard to prove that she's not from New Jersey. If I had grown up in Manhattan, would I have had the motivation to become a writer? Possibly not.

What's more, the older I get, the more I appreciate the things I once scorned about Fort Lee. On the one hand, it lacks all trace of charm. On the other hand, it's refreshingly unpretentious. Though I love city living, I get tired of the attitude that seems to permeate the very sidewalk.

Maybe that's why I still make the hourlong trip to Fort Lee from my home in Brooklyn every six months or so to visit my family dentist, Dr. Schneider. Actually, Dr. Schneider is semiretired now, but his practice has been taken over by an extremely capable former naval dentist named Dr. Jin. Last time I went in—for a new cap—I didn't have a ride back to the George Washington Bridge. It was almost closing time, so Dr. Jin was kind enough to drive me there. It's hard to imagine a New York dentist offering you a ride home.

As I made my way back to the city, I couldn't help but notice the decrepit two-story brick outline of the Tollgate motel, at the foot of the bridge. During the many years I have been passing through Fort Lee, en route to Leonia and elsewhere, I have never seen more than one car or truck parked in the Tollgate's sloping asphalt driveway. Reasonable hourly rates notwithstanding, I'm still mystified as to how the place manages to stay in business. But then, unlike the rest of us, Fort Lee has always kept its secrets well.

# TAKING THE NETS

## DAVID ROTH

EXIT 165

**W**e would stuff the bright packs right into our pockets. It was strictly Topps for baseball and football, but when I was shoplifting basketball cards I preferred the foil-covered Upper Deck packs. I remember the cards, too: slick white borders and big, bright action photography and the signature small, triangular hologram on the back. We'd walk uptown over frozen sidewalks and wood chips, past lumps of plowed snow grayed by car exhaust and heaped sagging on corners. We wound down our shortcuts of choice, cutting through the parking lots and half alleys of downtown Ridgewood, New Jersey, my hometown. We were on our way to Thrift Drug—which had been Woolworth's and would later become Rite Aid. We all walked in together, conspicuously, and headed straight for the back of the store, where the basketball and baseball and football cards were kept on a shelf. Once out of sight, we stole hungrily, quickly, then made our escape past the distracted teenagers and mysterious elderly women who made up Thrift Drug's permanent skeleton crew of a staff.

We ripped open the packs there in the store's back parking lot, in bright winter sunlight. The card companies of the era overproduced and overdistributed, and though we as kids read the Beckett price guides and studiously analyzed our portfolios—diversified by sport; I even lifted hockey cards—we didn't anticipate that a glut of those cards would eventually cut the bottom out from under our glossy, album-bound nest eggs. The cards are worth nothing now, or nothing more than whatever value their owners ascribe to them. My bottom line–oriented shoplifting buddies would sort out what were then the valuable cards and leave the rest in piles. That seemed wasteful to me, and strangely unkind. I couldn't do it. The thought of those forlorn stacks, made to be cared for by the very people who were deserting them there in the parking lot, made me sad.

So I kept everything, but I did not love all my basketball cards equally. I sorted through the cards I'd stolen and moved to the top of my stack all the cards that featured players from the New Jersey Nets. Their whole roster was there on those worthless glossy cards, the players caught in action wearing uniforms that look silly today—all tubular, too-bright '90s lettering and awkward piping. The haircuts are dated, overflamboyant—the high-top fades like pencil erasers, the odd drippy Jheri curl. Even the frozen movements of the players seem dated, as if people don't run or jump or smile like that anymore. But these were my Nets: their cards were valuable to me, even the end-of-the-bench Kurk Lees and Tate Georges and end-of-the-road Reggie Theuses and Eric "Sleepy" Floyds. Especially them.

My sad-sack hometown franchise would, I was sure, someday sneak off with something important and shock the world in the process. They looked ridiculous on their cards, maybe even then, but that can be a nice cover. No one suspected them, and no one suspected me, either. What I hoped they would take, and what I imagined I was taking on those afternoons at Thrift Drug, is still somewhat unclear to me. It sure wasn't the NBA Championship, which at that point was securely in the hands of Michael Jordan's Chicago Bulls, apparently in perpetuity. Making the playoffs would've been a nice start.

For the spindly sons of New Jersey—or at least for this one, so substandard in the things middle school deemed dear—much seemed impossible. At 98 pounds of conflict and need, I was an easy punch line. And so were my carelessly maligned state and its frankly crappy basketball team. Underdogs, underrated, all of us: if we were to succeed, we would have to do it through and around and over everyone and everything else. It was adolescent fatalism in fullest flower, but it was also the beginning of a New Jersey consciousness that would find its most passionate incarnation through my love of the Nets.

•  •  •

I understood New Jersey through my father. He grew up in Jersey City during the graft-intensive mayoralty of John V. Kenny, "The Little Guy." Both state and local politics were, at the time, corrupt in laughably low-rent ways—I recall here a story about a low-grade Jersey City pol riding around my father's neighborhood on a truck, yelling "Who troo da bomb, Louie?" through a bullhorn. But to hear my father tell the stories, it was authentically corrupt, and almost honest in that way, with even the rottenest politicians cognizant (I'm stretching) of the limits of unacceptable behavior. The idea that somehow our state's buggy, pollutant-belching political machine (chugging still) was also a treasured antique deserving of grudging maintenance was only the beginning of the seeming contradictions my father taught me. I wound up latching on to these contradictions as the things I loved most about the state.

The state was ugly but beautiful—you had to know where to look and what to look for, and know how to see that certain types of ugliness can be beautiful. The produce was, I was told, the best in the nation, the blueberries and the country corn and especially the round, red beefsteak tomatoes, but of course no one would ever know this, no one could get past the seemingly incongruous Garden State moniker. And the nickname did make sense, but couldn't compete with the state's self-defeating choice to run the main avenues of inter- and intrastate transit boldly through the distended, purpled musculature of the state's unbeautiful industry. No tomato could compete with the reek and ghoulish nighttime glow coming from the false cities of refineries along the turnpike south of Exit 15. But we knew what was what.

So: take the good with the bad, learn to love some unlovely

things, enjoy the tomatoes in season, and never forget where you're from. These lessons, all with attendant antitheses, were communicated through subtext on long car rides up and down from the shore or Grandma's house in Jersey City's Greenville neighborhood or along the small highways of Bergen and Hudson and Essex as my father drove me to my traveling team basketball games in the misshapen gyms of North Arlington and Rutherford and Wallington.

The Nets, to my eighth-grade mind, fit perfectly amid all this ugly beauty and surly charm. They had been, in my early youth, the worst team in the National Basketball Association and had posted some of the worst records in NBA history. The '87–88 team won nineteen of eighty-two games, under the tutelage of three very different, and presumably very patient, head coaches. The '89–90 team—the first one I really cared about—was even worse, finishing with seventeen wins. I will say this about that team: they actually were that bad, and possibly worse. I will say this also: I loved them.

In early middle school I started to be charmed by these losing Nets teams, with their thrift-store rosters wearing ill-fitting replicas of the old star-spangled ABA uniforms Dr. J had worn with the Nets in Long Island more than a decade earlier. The teams the Nets put out between 1987 and 1991 were so motley that any Jersey person—or any Jersey person who had grown up in the Jersey my father described, with that place's reflexive and defensive embrace of everything ugly as containing some germ of beauty—couldn't help but love them. They were comprised of charming drug addicts and gimpy vets and half-defective veterans of the NBA's satellite minor leagues and overmatched ex-schoolboy stars with scared looks on their faces. They were epitomized by one of the most universally reviled "stars" I ever saw play: Joe Barry Carroll, or, as I once heard him called by a fan far wittier than I was at age eleven, Joe Barely Cares.

JBC stood seven feet tall and had a smooth beard and, as I remember it, small, ironic eyes. He moved languorously, was frequently injured, and almost never spoke to the media. A decade earlier, he'd been a beautiful player: the first overall pick of the 1980 draft (later traded for Hall of Famers Kevin McHale and Robert Parish) and, after several high-scoring seasons with the Golden State Warriors, an All-Star in 1986. That was just a few years before coming to the Nets, but after being traded to New Jersey before the '88–89 season he seemed to switch onto a sleepy autopilot. He showed up and lobbed jump hooks and managed to lead the team in rebounding before succumbing to injury, but his drowsy demeanor drove fans wild with rage. I was eleven years old and ready to cheer for anyone taller than me, but far outnumbered by sputtering men with harsh opinions and their abashed, distracted wives and silent, confused kids. Those men hated Joe Barry Carroll. I understood little of it, but, in a half-deserted arena given over mostly to stubborn-to-a-fault season ticket holders and wild school groups shrieking and chanting in the far reaches of the upper section, I heard every jeer. I'm certain Joe Barry Carroll did, too. The Nets finally dealt him after a season and a half, acquiring an injured rookie guard named Michael Cutright who would never play in an NBA game. The trade didn't make the team better, but while it continued to lose, it also seemed to begin taking losing a bit more personally. It was the start of a new era.

At least for me, it was. I was in middle school and found myself more receptive to the idea of the underdog and, concurrently and for the first time, burning with resentment of those who seemed to lack sympathy for ungraceful strugglers. This was the beginning of what ultimately became a rather complete projection of myself onto the New Jersey Nets. My resentment toward those without Nets-love in their hearts was not class resentment—my parents both worked, the Roths did fine. It was just resentment of those I imagined weren't struggling as hard as I was and thus couldn't understand how singularly important and valid was the concurrent fight for respect waged simultaneously, on three fronts, by me, the post-JBC Nets, and New Jersey itself.

I envied the things that gave them the right to stay out of it—upper-body strength, clear minds and consciences and complexions, parents delighted to purchase expensive soccer shorts, parents who hadn't bequeathed the black gift of late-onset puberty. But I think I would've been able to get past all that if they hadn't laughed at my basketball team. These kids were my neighbors but became, to me, my opponents—the imagined ease of their lives was projected onto the slick New York Knicks, their team of choice. It was around this time that the Nets began to turn things around.

I, on the other hand, was not turning things around. By the winter of eighth grade I was hitting what counts as bottom for bourgeois twelve-year-olds in the North Jersey suburbs. I failed classes and sassed teachers; I stole not only cards but also baseball hats and used CDs and once either six or nine

Cadbury Creme Eggs. It was that old free-floating resentment again, the rage against an order that refused to allow me as many basketball cards as I wanted. And also, plain old acting out; fighting anything and everything, because I needed to. I would, eventually, get caught stealing, but that was some time off. For a brief, burning period, I was getting away with all this. I arrived home before my progress reports and diverted them. I had talking points prepared for the ones I let pass on to my parents. My basketball skills reached their peak—I spent what had been once been homework hours in playground games or wrapped up in a baroque simulated season that unfolded in my driveway—even as the rest of my life fell away. My jump shot became deadly; I learned to score (well, when playing alone) with my left hand. And I was something like a regular at Nets home games, thanks to friends' parents' largely unwanted company seats and a ticket package my father purchased before I started fucking up. I was never more passionate about them, and have never needed them as much as I did then.

So I was a regular, almost, but not a Brendan Byrne Arena quasi-celebrity like Tuffy—the cohost of WNYC's *Video Music Box*, who attended games with MTV's Ed Lover and often sang the pregame national anthem. I was almost affiliated, by dint of our ticket package location, with one Byrne notable: Johnny, a charming and energetic goofball who wore a Gilligan-style bucket cap and plaid shorts. Johnny sat above us in section 211 and led the derivative but undeniably effective chant that went "N-E-T-S, Nets Nets Nets" from the landing at the bottom of the section during strategic moments. Then he'd run, pumping and winded, back to his seat twenty-five rows up. Exhausted after streaking back up 211's steep stairs, Johnny would crash in our row, on the outside seat. We were having fun at the Byrne, and, for the first time in a long while, we were watching a team worth cheering for.

Years of losing had won the Nets high draft picks, and while Derrick Coleman (first overall pick in 1990) and Kenny Anderson (second overall in 1991) did not ever become great NBA players, they were an exciting, energized pair of young stars. Drazen Petrovic—a fierce, charismatic, beetle-browed Croatian scorer stolen from the end of the Portland Trail Blazers' bench via trade—emerged as one of the league's best shooters. And then there were the things that never quite broke right, suddenly breaking right—the perpetually pouty Chris Morris, a former lottery pick with great basketball talent and little apparent interest in basketball, suddenly kind of getting his shit together. Throw-in players like Chris Dudley and Terry Mills emerging as solid role players. (Dudley was a classic Net: a Yale-educated seven-footer who was the son of a former U.S. ambassador to Denmark, possessed of an on-court mean streak, patrician facial features, and a remarkable inability to make foul shots.) And here, somehow, was the most emblematic Net of all—JBC's replacement and NBA All-Punchline First Teamer Sam Bowie, a gimpy center forever infamous for having been drafted ahead of Michael Jordan (not, as it turned out, by New Jersey)—turning in a largely healthy and productive season in the middle.

They were a fun team—they tried hard, had players I loved, were coached by a memorably acerbic gnome named Bill Fitch, who would retire with more losses than any other coach in NBA history—and made the playoffs for the first time in six seasons. But my devotion to them was probably a bit much. Then, of course, it was indescribably important that the Nets succeed, with my help, and in so doing prove the things that I imagined their success would prove. But in retrospect, that burden of righteous justification seems an awful lot—too much—to ask of a sports team. The conflicting projections—struggling adolescent me onto the underrated and disrespected Nets and the Nets back onto me; the Nets onto New Jersey and back again; New Jersey onto me and me onto New Jersey—wound up producing an impenetrable blaze of adolescent overage.

I clung to the Nets ferociously, with an intensity of affinity rivaled only by my more ostentatiously bad habits. I treasured the subrituals and details of going to games—my lucky black Nets cap, walks through the reeking turnpike overpass from the Giants Stadium parking lot to the Byrne's, the weird encroachment of the swamp along Paterson Plank Road, and especially the burgers with my father in a smoky roadside hovel called Steve's Sizzling Steaks in Carlstadt. A lot of what I drew from the experience, though, began and ended with screaming. Cheering loudly was a more cathartic expression of the needs I had at the time, and raised fewer legal and moral questions, than shoplifting. In time, my love for the Nets supplanted my shoplifting. Whereas racking was furtive and internal and almost private (we spoke afterward, but my partners and I kept solemn silence during our runs), Nets games were loud and big and offered a community of people who wanted the same things I did. And, as I vocally defended the honor of all the things I thought the Nets meant, the games gave me the opportunity to focus and turn outward the resentment that made me such an impressive adolescent screw-up. My weapon was a righteous, flaming sword of an adolescent voice.

I chewed out front-runners, the opportunists who inhabited the lowest circle of my sport-infidel hierarchy. I had particular venom reserved for Jersey-born Knicks fans. At one game, a surprise victory the Nets stole from the Knicks (I still have the ticket stub), I got into a shouting match with a mean-looking, overweight lady dipped in Knicks logo wear. It was a profoundly inappropriate thing on both of our parts. I remember her instigating it, but memory can be opportunistic that way. Either way, she was a grown woman and certainly should not have been yelling at me through shards of cigarette teeth and anger, "When was the last time you [i.e., the Nets] won anything? *Never! Never!*" I dismissed her, probably profanely, with an admonition to go back to Kearny, an industrial ethnic-white Newark suburb that, to my unconsciously elitist adolescent brain, seemed the sort of place a woman like that might live.

If she had been from New York, I told myself, if these Knicks fans had come over from unimaginable New York to cheer for their guys, then that was kind of okay. But to be from New Jersey and not cheer for the Nets was beneath contempt. I don't know that I could've articulated this to the woman, but what I think I wanted to say to her was not, really, a rebuttal. Of course we'd never won anything, I (didn't know that I) wanted to say. You, too, all of us here, we've never won anything. That's why we scream, that's why we care so much. Here was my revolutionary Jersey consciousness, live and loud. And I wasn't fully wrong, I don't think. No, lady, we'd never won anything. No one is going to let us win anything—I was sure of this—because we're small and terrible things once washed up on our beaches and our highways look infected and our cities are empty sockets and our politics an oil slick six decades wide.

And it doesn't matter: pull your fucking weight, or never understand that it's actually the right thing for us to fight for recognition and a little respect, which is not really too much to ask. Never understand that when it came down to it you would never be able to change yourself enough to seem as if you weren't from here. Never understand that there's no shame in being what you are, which is someone born into New Jersey, with New Jersey in turn born into you. Understand that, embrace that, and understand how close that is to the heart of being in and of this place, or go back to whatever dark part of it you come from.

Three years ago the Nets were sold by the contentious gaggle of soft-faced millionaires who had owned them for most of my lifetime. The team had recently become very good, following some sour seasons after the passing on of my Nets— Drazen Petrovic was killed in a car accident in Germany; Chris Morris and Derrick Coleman and later Kenny Anderson grew uninterested; Bowie got hurt again; Dudley left as a free agent. A decade's worth of teams, with a few exceptions, were anonymous and submediocre. The acquisition of the genius point guard Jason Kidd in 2002 and some more good draft picks brought about the best Nets teams of my lifetime, or anyone else's. In 2003 and 2004, New Jersey made it all the way to the NBA finals.

The new Nets, whom at first I hardly recognized but soon embraced as demonstrating the spirit of my old friends (alongside much better team defense), were then purchased by a New York real estate magnate named Bruce Ratner. No basketball fan—the previous owners weren't, either—Ratner plans to move the Nets to Brooklyn, where they will play in one of those enormous, shiny crashed-UFO Frank Gehry designs that never quite seem to get built. The Nets arena will be the centerpiece of Ratner's redevelopment of a wide stretch of land between the neighborhoods of Fort Greene and Prospect Heights in Brooklyn. Controversies surround the sale, but it seems, as I write this, to be going forward despite a well-organized and growing neighborhood opposition to Ratner's extensive redevelopment plans. The formerly tightfisted Ratner has started to pay his star players star salaries, and it appears that the team he will take to Brooklyn in 2007 or 2008 will still be pretty good. Until then, they will keep on in Jersey.

Tickets sell fairly well at the old Brendan Byrne Arena, which is now Continental Airlines Arena, but there's a last-day-of-school feel to the game experience now. The public address announcer, it seems, has been told to stop saying the state's name. This probably has something to do with re-branding the team, but there's nevertheless a strange beat when the announcer introduces "your . . . Nets" before every game. My Nets are the New Jersey Nets. It's strange to think of them not being that. I have been avoiding doing so and plan on continuing that.

Five years ago, I also left New Jersey for Brooklyn, but I go back for games when I can—it's both easier and cheaper to get to Nets games via mass transit from New York than it is to get there from anywhere in Jersey. I watch games back in Ridgewood around Christmas with my old Nets game crew. Only one of them, Ned, now a sportswriter in New Hampshire, lived in Jersey during the last basketball season. I went to a game with him at the end of last year courtesy of his father, who had secured some tickets through his office. Approaching the arena by bus is almost poignant these days—like so many of the forlorn constructions along Paterson Plank Road, it's easy to imagine the old Brendan Byrne as a ruin, decrepit and overgrown back into swamp. Of course, I wouldn't mind that. Read Philip Roth or William Carlos Williams or Frederick Reiken, listen to Bruce Springsteen or the Wrens or my dad: New Jersey appreciates a good ruin.

The ticket lady said to me, "You know these are super-duper seats, right," when I showed her my ticket at that game. I didn't know. I had never gone in through that particular gate before, but I knew the seats were supposed to be better than any in which I'd ever sat. I looked down at the price: $700, which is indeed super-duper. Ned's father had gotten his tickets directly from the NBA, and the seats were on the floor, separated from the action by just one row of folding chairs, luxuriously upholstered in the arena's familiar woven purple plastic. I found that everything is included for those with $700 seats: free beers and free soda and free popcorn and free hot dogs and free gummy chicken fingers. We ate and we drank and we sat, this once, where the players could hear us yell.

But of course it was different. I'm older, and need these Nets less. Ned yelled at the Sixers—the Nets needed to beat them to secure a playoff spot and did so thanks to great performances by Jason Kidd and another newly acquired star, Vince Carter. I did my best to do so as well, but there was something disorienting about being so close. We were sitting a row behind the Nets' most famous new co-owner—the rapper Jay-Z, sporting a diamond-encrusted watch the size and brightness of a pancaked chandelier—and a row from the basketball game itself. At one point near the end of the first half Bruce Ratner himself walked by, and I saw that he was not a villain but a familiar nebbishy New York swell, another goof in a pink oxford and blue blazer. Even Jay-Z, so casual and cool in his videos, looked puffy and self-important. The people seated around us didn't pay much attention to the goings-on in the game. Photographers crouched and leaned under the basket stanchions, taking shots for basketball cards that would enumerate and freeze these players for another generation. The players occasionally cursed in frustration and the manic coaches shrilled out instructions from the bench, but by and large, it was oddly quiet down there. It was a good crowd at a good game, but the arena didn't fill with noise the way I remember it once having done. And, while this seems strange to say about men so large, the players actually seemed rather small.

# ACKNOWLEDGMENTS

One of the pleasures of working on this anthology was discovering how many New Jersey enthusiasts were eager to help me realize this collection, offer words of encouragement, or simply talk Jersey.

For their assistance in the early conceptual stages of this project, I must thank Marissa Walsh and Alicia Brooks. Elizabeth Searle, Lisa Dierbeck, Karen Auerbach, Hannah Pfeifle, and Felicia Sullivan (along with other members of the Old Girls' Club) were instrumental in helping me lure such an impressive list of contributors. Jeff Sharlet and Peter Manseau advised on a number of writerly matters. Tom Bissell was consulted on the cover. My dear friend Paul Morris brought about crucial initial connections, and was generous, as always, in lending time and energy on my behalf.

I am so thankful that Elizabeth Kaplan, agent extraordinaire, thrilled to the book idea as soon as it landed on her desk. And, quite frankly, there could have been no other editor for this anthology: Amanda Patten (Exit 8A: Cranbury) was not only an enthusiastic advocate and astute reader but a true collaborator. Had we known each other back in our college days at Rutgers, I probably would have begun this project that much sooner.

For the kind of sustenance only longtime friendship can provide, I want to thank Dana Levin, Karolin Shoikhet-Obregon, and Natalia Vayner. Without Sonya Bekkerman by my side for over twenty-five years, I may have never dared to be a writer.

My deep love and gratitude go to my parents, Mark and Gina, who yanked me out of the Soviet Union only so I could spend the rest of my life writing about it. My sister Elizabeth, who at age sixteen has already completed several novels, continues to inspire me. I want to thank my grandparents and my aunt for their presence in my life, and my paternal grandparents, who are no longer living, but who, I think, would be proud.

I'm not exaggerating when I say this is my husband's, Adam Lowenstein's, book just as much as it is mine. It was his native pride in the Garden State that fueled this undertaking. Over the years, he has shared with me his affection for Springsteen and Little Steven, Wawa food markets, Long Beach Island, and soft-serve vanilla ice cream on the boardwalk. I feel lucky to traverse bridges and tunnels with him.

# ABOUT THE CONTRIBUTORS

**Jonathan Ames** is the author of three novels, *I Pass like Night*, *The Extra Man*, and *Wake Up, Sir!*, and three collections of essays, *What's Not to Love?*, *My Less Than Secret Life*, and *I Love You More than You Know*. He grew up in Oakland, New Jersey, and is a graduate of Princeton University.

**Gaiutra Bahadur** covers immigration for *The Philadelphia Inquirer*. In her decade as a reporter, she has filed stories from a fortressed hotel in Baghdad and the pink-domed state capitol in Austin, Texas. Her book reviews and travelogues have appeared in numerous publications, including *Ms.*, *Salon*, and the Indian magazine *Outlook Traveler*. Gaiutra is a graduate of Yale University and the Columbia University Graduate School of Journalism.

**Christian Bauman** is the author of the novels *Voodoo Lounge*, *The Ice Beneath You*, and the forthcoming *In Hoboken*; a regular contributor to NPR's *All Things Considered*; and an editor-at-large for IdentityTheory.com.

He grew up amid the shrinking farmlands of Hunterdon County, New Jersey. Although he never actually had a legal residence east of I-287, he used to work Tuesday nights at Maxwell's on Eleventh and Washington, and was a founding member of the almost-band Camp Hoboken—he hopes these two points may be enough to at least grant him an entrance interview with Saint Peter.

**Joshua Braff** was born and raised in New Jersey. He studied education at New York University and graduated in 1991. In 1997 he received an MFA in creative writing/fiction from Saint Mary's College in Moraga, California. His first novel, *The Unthinkable Thoughts of Jacob Green,* was nominated for a 2005 Quill Award and also made the *San Francisco Chronicle* best-seller list. A new short story of his has just been published in an anthology called *The Encyclopedia of Exes* (Crown). He has also published short fiction in national literary journals, including *The Alaska Quarterly Review* and *River Styx.* He lives in Oakland, California, with his wife and two children.

**Kathleen DeMarco,** a lecturer in the Creative Writing Program at the University of Pennsylvania, is the author of the novels *Cranberry Queen* and *The Difference Between You and Me.* A native of Hammonton, New Jersey, she has recently moved to Moorestown, New Jersey, with her husband and two sons after fifteen years of living in New York City.

**Lauren Grodstein** is the author of the novel *Reproduction Is the Flaw of Love* and *The Best of Animals,* a collection of stories. A native of Haworth, New Jersey, she is a professor of English at Rutgers-Camden.

**Cathi Hanauer** is the author of two novels, *Sweet Ruin* and *My Sister's Bones,* and the editor of the *New York Times* best-selling essay collection *The Bitch in the House: 26 Women Tell the Truth About Sex, Solitude, Work, Motherhood and Marriage.* Her articles and essays have appeared in numerous magazines, including *Elle, O, Self, Glamour, Parenting, Redbook, Child,* and *Mademoiselle.* She was the monthly books columnist for both *Glamour* and *Mademoiselle* and wrote the monthly advice column "Relating" in *Seventeen* magazine for seven years. She grew up in West Orange, New Jersey, and now lives in western Massachusetts with her family. Visit her website at www.cathihanauer.com.

**James Kaplan** is a novelist, journalist, essayist, and critic. He has written more than a hundred major profiles for such magazines as *The New Yorker, The New York Times Magazine, Vanity Fair, Esquire,* and *New York.* His 1998 novel, *Two Guys from Verona,* chosen by *The New York Times* as one of its Notable Books of the Year, is being developed as a movie by Hart-Sharp Entertainment. In 2002 Kaplan coauthored the autobiography of John McEnroe, *You Cannot Be Serious,* which was an international best seller (and number one on the *New York Times* list). His most recent book, *Dean & Me: (A Love Story)*, cowritten with Jerry Lewis and published by Doubleday in October 2005, was a *New York Times* bestseller as well. He is currently at work on a definitive biography of Frank Sinatra, also for Doubleday. He lives in Westchester, New York, with his wife and three sons.

**Elizabeth M. Keenan** is the coauthor of *Synchronicity*, a full-length play that had two sold-out runs at the Producers' Club in New York City. A graduate of Marymount Manhattan College, she now works at a major publishing house and lives in Manhattan. She is a regular contributor to the online magazine *New York Inquirer*. Currently she is at work on her first novel.

**Caroline Leavitt** is the author of eight novels, including *Girls in Trouble*, a BookSense selection. The recipient of a New York Foundation of the Arts Award and a National Magazine Award nominee, she is still deliriously happy to be living in Hoboken with her husband, the writer Jeff Tamarkin, and their young son, Max. Her website is www.carolineleavitt.com.

**Caren Lissner** is the author of the humorous novel *Carrie Pilby* (2003) and has published humor pieces in *The New York Times* and *Philadelphia Inquirer*. Full-time, she serves as the editor in chief of the *Hudson Reporter* newspaper group in Hoboken, New Jersey. She grew up in Freehold and lives in Hoboken. More of her writing can be found at www.carenlissner.com.

**Adam Lowenstein** is an associate professor of English and film studies at the University of Pittsburgh. He is the author of *Shocking Representation: Historical Trauma, National Cinema, and the Modern Horror Film* (Columbia University Press, 2005) as well as essays published in a variety of film journals and anthologies. Among his current projects is a memoir concerning his lifelong enthusiasm for horror movies. He grew up in Highland Park, New Jersey.

**Askold Melnyczuk**'s last novel, *Ambassador of the Dead,* was a *Los Angeles Times* Best Book of 2002. A founding editor of *Agni,* he teaches at UMass Boston and at the Bennington Graduate Writing Seminars. His fourth book, *House of Widows,* will appear next year.

**Tom Perrotta** grew up in Garwood, New Jersey. He's the author of four novels—*Little Children, Joe College, Election,* and *The Wishbones*—and a story collection, *Bad Haircut. Election* was made into an acclaimed 1999 movie directed by Alexander Payne, starring Matthew Broderick and Reese Witherspoon. *Little Children* has recently been made into a movie directed by Todd Field, starring Kate Winslet. Perrotta, who lives in Massachusetts with his wife and two children, has taught writing at Yale and Harvard, and written nonfiction for *GQ, Rolling Stone,* and *The New York Times Book Review.*

**Frederick Reiken**'s first novel, *The Odd Sea,* won the Hackney Literary Award and was selected by both *Booklist* and *Library Journal* as one of the best first novels of 1998.

His second novel, *The Lost Legends of New Jersey,* was a *New York Times* Notable Book of 2000 and a *Los Angeles Times* Best Book of the Year. His short fiction has appeared in *The New Yorker* and other publications. He is a professor of writing and literature at Emerson College and lives with his wife in western Massachusetts. During his childhood, he lived for varying amounts of time in the following New Jersey towns: Orange, Livingston, Nutley, Fort Lee, Mendham, Summit, Short Hills, West Orange, South Orange, and Boonton.

**Lucinda Rosenfeld** is the author of the novels *What She Saw . . .* (Random House, 2000) and *Why She Went Home* (Random House, 2004). She grew up in Leonia, New Jersey, and now lives in Brooklyn.

**David Roth** is a writer from New Jersey who lives in New York. His fiction has appeared in *Post Road*; his nonfiction and essays have appeared, almost as if by magic, in *Slate, The Wall Street Journal Online, The New Republic Online* and in *The Independent.* He also writes text for the backs of baseball, basketball, and football cards for Topps.

**Dani Shapiro**'s most recent books include the novels *Black & White* and *Family History.* She is also the author of the best-selling memoir *Slow Motion.* Her work has appeared in *The New Yorker, Granta, The New York Times Magazine, Elle, O, House & Garden, Tin House, Ploughshares,* and *Bookforum,* among others. She is currently visiting writer at Wesleyan University.

# CREDITS

"The Family Farm" copyright © 2007 by Kathleen DeMarco

"Rose of the Jersey Shore" copyright © 2000 by Jonathan Ames. First published in *What's Not to Love? The Adventures of a Mildly Perverted Young Writer*. Used by permission.

"Notes on Camden" copyright © 2007 by Lauren Grodstein

"A Rumble and a Scream" copyright © 2007 by Caren Lissner

"Suburban Legends" copyright © 2007 by Elizabeth Keenan

"New Jersey: The Movie" copyright © 2007 by Adam Lowenstein

"Straight Outta Garwood" copyright © 2005 by Tom Perrotta. First published in *The Star-Ledger* (Newark). Used by permission.

"The Venice of New Jersey" copyright © 2007 by Askold Melnyczuk